Anthony Trollope

An Annotated Bibliography

Anthony Trollope

An Annotated Bibliography

Of Periodical Works By and About Him

In the United States and Great Britain to 1900

by

Anne K. Lyons

The Penkevill Publishing Company
Greenwood, Florida

Copyright ©
1985
Anne K. Lyons

ISBN 0–913283–04–5
Printed in the United States of America

For Ruth and John Kearns

Unlike many Trollopian characters, they have always been *much* better than they should be.

Acknowledgements

This book owes its existence to a number of people other than the compiler. The most fundamental contributors are, of course, Anthony Trollope and his faithful readers and reviewers of a century ago; these are followed by the careful bibliographers between then and now, especially Professor Houghton and the *Wellesley Index* collaborators.

More immediately, I would like to thank James R. Kincaid, who suggested this project to me and who provided encouragement and helpful suggestions from idea to completed manuscript. Especially, I would like to thank Gladys Weibel Goldman, to whose care and garnering instincts we owe the extensive collection of Victorian periodicals in the University of Colorado library.

I am grateful, finally, to my family, who helped in many and various ways, and who endured so gracefully the demands which my work placed on them.

CONTENTS

1
Introduction

17
Articles About Trollope

125
Articles By Trollope

153
Bibliography

155
Appendix A
Periodicals Surveyed for this Bibliography

157
Appendix B
Entries Cited by Works Discussed

159
Appendix C
Entries Cited by Selected Topics

161
Appendix D
Entries Cited by Authors

162
Appendix E
Entries Cited by Publication

Introduction

Anthony Trollope authored seventy-one published books — fiction, nonfiction, and drama — and numerous articles in periodicals and newspapers, and was during his lifetime an enormously popular author. His audience's range of education and taste was extraordinarily wide. Sales of Trollope's works occasionally rivalled even those of Dickens. Thus, allusions and reviews appeared in every sort of periodical, in an era which was the heyday of periodial publication.

Because of this "ubiquity" of Trollope references, compiling a complete bibliography of this material is a virtual impossibility. The difficulties attendant upon assembling a systematic partial bibliography are, as previous compilers of these have explained, enormously taxing. Thus, such works are generally characterized by their lacunae and limitations.

The first widely accessible bibliography of Trollope's works was published in 1925 by Mary Leslie Irwin. Ms. Irwin cites as her chief source, "four numbers of Mr. F. W. Faxon's Bulletin of Bibliography, running from May, 1924, to December, 1925."[1] She lists primary and secondary works published both in England and abroad, including those in translation. She includes lectures given by Trollope, notices, descriptions and dispositions of known photographs, manuscripts, and first editions. Perhaps because her scope is so wide, attempting to encompass all "Trollopiana," Irwin's bibliography has many gaps. She missed some fairly obvious reviews, for example, in the *Westminster Review*. Her notes are rather sketchy and sometimes unclear. She does not list most of his early contributions to *St. Paul's*. It is, nonetheless, helpful as an early indication of sources of Trollope criticism.

Michael Sadleir's bibliography[2] of early editions of Trollope's works was published in 1928; this book has very detailed descriptions, including pictures in some cases, of the early editions, and seems designed particularly, even exclusively, for book collectors. Margaret Lavington's bibliography of Trollope first editions appears in Escott's *Anthony*

Trollope: His Work, Associates, and Literary Originals.[3] She includes physical descriptions of the volumes and notes on the business details of publication.

Thus, only one bibliography of nineteenth century criticism has been published (Irwin's), and it is not annotated. Two bibliographies of twentieth century criticism have been compiled: Philip Holcomb's unpublished dissertaion (University of Colorado, 1972) which describes 500 items published between 1920 and 1968, and John Olmstead and Jeffrey Welch's annotated bibliography covering the years, 1925-1975.[4]

Two studies of Trollope's reputation, based on surveys of criticism, exist. Iva Jones' unpublished dissertation, "A Study of the Literary Reputation of Anthony Trollope, 1847-1953," (Ohio State University, 1953), depends very heavily on Irwin's bibliography and is marked throughout by the writer's interposition of her personal agreement with or disapproval of the critics she surveys.

A Century of Trollope Criticism, by Rafael Helling[5] is not a helpful book for scholars. He announces in the introduction that he will deal more extensively with positive than with negative criticism, largely "because appreciative interpretations are more useful generally."[6] In quoting from journals, Helling frequently cites only the title and year as identification. His bibliography lists the periodicals he consulted by title only.

A much more helpful work for those interested in Trollope criticism is the Critical Heritage series' volume on Trollope, edited by Donald Smalley.[7] This volume provides the original texts of reviews and excerpts of 253 criticial notices, letters, and reviews of Trollope's fiction. The greatest number of selections are taken from daily or weekly British and American publications between 1847 and 1888, sources not easily accessible today. Smalley does not include reviews of Trollope's many non-fiction works, and many of the items have been abridged to allow their inclusion in the collection; however, they serve to give an accurate account of the reception accorded Trollope's fiction by his contemporaries.

The Wellesley Index to Victorian Periodicals, 1824-1900,[8] which is still in progress, is certainly one of the major recent contributions to Victorian studies, particularly to bibliographic research. This work, under the editorship of Walter Houghton, has thus far surveyed and catalogued the contents of thirty-five major nineteenth century British periodicals from 1824 through 1900. Volume IV, which will add thirteen journals to this number, is expected in 1984. In addition to listing all of the contents of these publications, the *Wellesley Index* identified the authors of a very sizeable percentage of the articles. The detective work required for this identification was nothing short of heroic; as Houghton explains in the introduction, "most articles and stories in the Victorian periodicals were anonymous or pseudonymous — before 1870 about 97%, for the whole period about 90%.[9] The value, then, of the *Index* is difficult to exaggerate; it shortens dramatically the time required of researchers of the period, not only in literature but in virtually any aspect of Victorian culture. The *Index* does include in appendices an index of authors and one of general topics; it does not, however, indicate the contents of such items as book review columns, articles on "Recent Fiction," and the like.

David Skilton's *Anthony Trollope and His Contemporaries*[10] is also very helpful in locating early reviews of Trollope's works, and in identifying the authors of those in the *Athenaeum* (he was allowed access to the original files of that journal). His bibliography includes reviews not listed elsewhere, and he surveyed a number of periodicals not included in the *Wellesley Index*.

This volume attempts to fill in some of the gaps left by the preceding works. It is an annotated bibliography of items either by or about Trollope and appearing in periodicals in England, Scotland, Ireland, and the United States between 1847 and the end of 1900.[11]

The nineteenth century brought for millions of people an increase in both literacy and leisure. The enormous number of periodicals and reviews which were begun in this period served both interests. Although many magazines were short-lived, many others survived and flourished for decades. Politics, religious questions, general information, and reviews crowd the pages of many of them; as a rule, these periodicals had a greater variety of serious reading matter than do their counterparts today — suggesting an audience at least as hungry for opinion and information as for entertainment. There are frequent remarks in many of these magazines about the general obligation of people to understand such topics as marriage customs in the Near East, travel problems on the Isthmus of Panama, religious questions, agricultural methods, and other topics; these sorts of topics today would be treated more as curiosities than as requirements for the average citizen's stock of information.

The very plethora of such ephemeral reading material contributed to the difficulties for later researchers. Magazines were not, for the most part, preserved in many places, and they were not always accurately or systematically indexed when they were kept. At present no annotated bibliography exists of these materials; because of the volume of Trollope criticism that does exist, an annotated survey of articles about Trollope's non-fiction as well as his fiction should prove valuable. Because Trollope himself wrote for periodicals, not only reviewing books but also speaking on a wide variety of other topics, serious and light, it seems useful to have an account of that work. This bibliography should be a resource for researchers who have not the time, nor the library facilities, nor perhaps the inclination, to try to read everything in order to determine which items will be helpful for their projects. Further, since the periodicals surveyed here may reasonably be regarded as major book-reviewing organs of their era, the work will illustrate the general tenor of English and American literary criticism of the latter nineteenth century.

It is with the last feature that I have become fascinated in the course of compiling this volume. Certainly, the Victorian period, as any other, had a wider range of taste and value systems than an "overview" can fully take account of; however, there are frequently recurring references by reviewers to explicit and assumed values. Fiction, it is tacitly agreed, is a form of art. The dictum inherited from Longinus, by way of Sidney and Johnson, that art has two functions – to delight and to instruct – seems to have been held almost universally by reviewers of the second half of the nineteenth century. By and large, these reviewers also perceived art as a form of communication, created for an audience; it is not an experiment for its own sake, nor is it a form of self-expression. That a piece of literature should contain a "message" is virtually never called into question.

About the exact nature of the message there is some variety of opinion, although the great majority of reviewers were certain that it should be unmistakably moral — 'the sermons of our time,' as Trollope remarked in a speech. About the most suitable — that is, convincing — way of framing the message, there is greater disparity of views.

Most critics seemed to favor a modern-day, "realistic" setting and problem, though they frequently praised the "fifty years ago" settings of George Eliot's novels, or the even earlier ones of Scott. Relatively few critics before the 1880s were comfortable with out and out fantasy or with what they considered "exotic."

David Skilton describes the attitude of the middle and upper classes — the reading public of Trollope's time — as clearly derived from Dr. Johnson's prescriptions in the *Rambler*; there he pointed out that, while vice must appear in fiction, if the fiction is to imitate life (as it should), vice should always be presented as disgusting; "the young, the ignorant, and the idle" who read, use their reading material as "lectures on conduct, and introductions into life."[12] The problem central to the critical treatment of literature is evident here — how to balance the two major requirements of realism and moral didacticism. For the writer of fiction, this question became one of how to achieve the desired effects of delight and instruction; for the reviewer, our point of focus here, it is how to weigh the claims of edification and credibility in evaluating a novel. Evil must appear clearly recognizable as evil, and must be appropriately punished; on the other hand, it must be seen as believable, understandable, and — to some extent — sympathetic. Reviewer Geraldine Jewsbury expresses the difficulty posed by the latter requirement quite clearly in her review for the *Athenaeum* of *The Three Clerks*: she "wonders" whether the reader should be induced to care so much for Alaric Tudor, whose ambition outstrips his ethics; she notes with approval that his final punishment is fully adequate to his crime. One of the reviewers of *Sir Harry Hotspur of Humblethwaite* finds that novel, because of sympathetic evil characters, unsuitable for young people to read, but he suggests that mothers would be well advised to read it for the lesson available to them on the dangers to children of over-fond parents.

The reviewers of *Orley Farm* all notice that the author solicits sympathy for Lady Mason, despite the fact that she is clearly guilty; the anonymous reviewer of *The Saturday Review* remarks that *The Claver-*

ings "consoles us" in the end because Julia Ongar is punished just to the correct degree, no less and no more than she deserves.

Another difficulty the Victorians faced in dealing with fictive evil was caused by the different moral standards implicitly demanded of different social classes. It was not altogether unexpected that there would be prostitutes, alcoholics, cheats, and other unsavory types among the lower classes and among foreigners. Young readers did not apparently take such characters seriously, or consider them as possible models or correct interpreters of life. Thus, they could be disposed of without the assiduous care for justice; they could even be treated sympathetically, so long as they did not assume leadership in the main plot of a novel.

This latitude, though it seems to have been general, was not universally accepted even in Trollope's time, He notes in an 1867 article in *Temple Bar* that he was aware that many parents insisted on reading even the daily newspaper themselves, and removing sections which might be occasions of scandal or bad example, before allowing their "young people," especially their daughters, read it. Certainly such parents would read fiction, also, before allowing their children to do so.

For the most part, however, the reviewers served as the screening committee for concerned parents, and reviews not infrequently remark on the "suitability" of a certain work for young people. In the *Saturday Review*'s notice of *Lotta Schmidt,* for example, the writer notes with some satisfaction the "the most careful mother need not make a pioneer excursion among Mr. Trollope's pages" before allowing her daughters to read them.[13]

That reviewers, by and large, accepted the differing moral sensibilities of different classes is quite evident in an overview of the reviews of the time. The writers were themselves mostly members of the middle-class establishment and accepted its value system. For these people, respectability or gentility included both moral integrity and adherence to social conventions that were perceived as derivative of moral integrity. Keeping one's word was an essential part of this code. An honorable person did not change his or her mind about a promise to marry any more than one did about a promise to repay money owed. The moral and social became equally commanding rules for the reading class, and an offense against one code is virtually identical in weight with an offense against the other. For the lower classes, not brought up to understand this system, behavior was not expected to follow it. "Vulgar" is an epithet of the middle classes, used indiscriminately to describe lower class or morally repugnant people or acts.

An example of this understanding at work can be seen in the reviews of *The Vicar of Bulhampton*. No reviewer objected to the presence, or even the prominence, of Carrie Brattle, a prostitute and the daughter of a miller. Nor is her depiction as both beautiful and extremely sympathetic criticized. In the same novel, the heroine, Mary Lowther, twice breaks engagements to marry, both times clearly for reasons of conscience; in the end she marries happily. Margaret Oliphant, herself a novelist, says tersely in her review that "the less we hear about such people, the better off we are."[14]

Another reviewer of *The Vicar of Bulhampton* passes rather lightly over a father's cheating his son of an inheritance and wasting it, but thinks it seriously wrong for the son "to call his father a swindler and a liar to his face." Permitting this son to marry the heroine seems to the reviewer dangerously close to rewarding someone who clearly broke the commandment to honor father and mother.[15]

The Way We Live Now is condemned by two reviewers because a swindler seems to be the hero; one of these chastises the author for not having a prominent virtuous character to serve as a foil, and notes disparagingly that Trollope seems actually to like people who border on "the outlaw class."

Trollope's heroines, several of whom change their minds after promising to marry, are regularly criticzed for being defended or justified by the author. Of all the reviews included here of *Can You Forgive Her?* that written by Henry James for the *Nation* is alone in suggesting that the title inflates and exaggerates the seriousness of Alice Vavasor's actions. He alone sees Glencora as a more important and more interesting figure. This fact can be largely attributed to James's nationality — American — and his consequently being outside Trollope's primary audience.

Some reviewers object so strongly to characters and episodes as to wish them completely out of a book; this is the case with the residents of the boarding house in Burton Crescent, where the luckless Johnny Eames stayed. Although none of those characters triumphs in any way, their very presence in *The Small House at Allington* is condemned because of their "vulgarity," a term encompassing their tactlessness, greed, dishonesty, and class all at once. The Lucinda Roanoke courtship and near-marriage episode is wished out of *The Eustace Diamonds,* and the Conway Dalrymple episodes are noted as marring the otherwise very exceptional *The Last Chronicle of Barset.*

By the clear placement of his sympathies in his novels, Trollope the novelist indicates that he did not completely share his reviewer's insistence on respectability at all costs. As a reviewer himself, he makes clear his lack of squeamishness in dealing with evil. In the midst of a rather heated public controversy reflected in the *Times* over the presentation of "Formosa," a popular comedy by Don Boucicault about a contented prostitute, he wrote sorting out the issues involved.

After describing the various points of view which have been expressed on the matter (i.e., the protest of many citizens at such a show being performed, the producer's and manager's defense that they may show whatever will draw crowds), Trollope insists that there is nothing inherently immoral about writing (or producing, or acting in, or going to see) a play about a prostitute. Almost anything in common human experience is legitimate material for art. However, he continues, this particular play is bad, because it is untrue. The life of a prostitute is in fact a very sad, miserable, sometimes tragic one — it is not a comedy.[16] This work should not be produced because it is bad art. He insists on the *moral* obligations of writers, producers, and publishers not to promulgate untruth. Popular demand is an issue after the fact, and does not have any bearing on the issue of morality.

It is quite significant that in a discussion on the morality of a piece of art, Trollope brings up the issue of truth to reality; for this is the other hallmark of literary judgment in the nineteenth century.

There was a fascination, even a reverence, for "the real" among the Victorians, particularly in the third quarter of the century. The rise of empirical science to a position of eminence, seen in the writings of people such as Huxley and Darwin, certainly supported such an attitude. Futhermore, in an age of transition[17] such as the Victorians recognized theirs to be, the notion of certainty or of the verifiable is strongly appealing. The tremendous popularity of such diverse kinds of solid reality as represented by the exhibits at the Crystal Palace in 1861 and the pictures that anyone with a camera could produce bear witness to the high value placed on the real.

A glance at the titles of books published in this period shows the importance of this sense of reality even in fiction. Typical of such titles are the following: *Realities: a Tale,* by Eliza Linton (1850); *Miriam Sedley: a Tale of Real Life,* by Lady Bulwer-Lytton (1851); *A History of Henry Esmond, Esq. . . . Written by Himself,* by Thackeray (1852); *Scenes of Clerical Life,* by George Eliot (1858); and *The Arlingtons: Sketches from Life* (1866). These are but a small sampling of works which, in title or subtitle, claim to be true to life.

Not only did many authors promise pictures of reality in their titles; they were highly pleased when readers and/or reviewers indicated that their plots and characters were convincing. The letters of George Eliot, for example, contain many instances of her expression of delight at compliments on her realism.[18]

In his *Autobiography,* Trollope indicates his pleasure at the account Hawthorne gave of his work as "just as real as if some giant had hewn a great lump out of the earth and put it under a glass case, with all its inhabitants going about their daily business and not suspecting that they were being made a show of."[19] The extent of his happiness with this remark is seen in Trollope's having quoted it in full in the *Autobiography,* an uncharacteristic act. Hawthorne has, Trollope continues, "describe[d] with wonderful accuracy the purport that I have ever had in view of my writing."[20] Trollope then remarks in some detail on his sense of the importance of realism and plausibility in his writing; it must be real if it is to be an effective moral teacher, which he feels is the other primary aim of literature.

Not only was realism of great import to Trollope in his own writing; it was also a characteristic he noticed when commenting on others' work. As a reviewer for *The Fortnightly Review* and *St. Paul's Magazine,* he directed his harshest criticism at those works he found unrealistic. He notes of Mario's *The Red Shirt,* purportedly a biographical account of Garibaldi and his followers by one of them, that the narrative seems quite improbable – finally, it is "a bad book." Of *The Rose of Cheriton,* an anti-drink tract in the form of a story, he is careful to note that he is personally opposed to alcoholism and thus sympathetic to the writer's purpose, but that this cautionary tale is so improbable that it should never have been printed. In his review of *Lothair,* he accuses Disraeli of deliberately writing badly, as nothing else could account for such a hopelessly unrealistic plot.

In an article he wrote three years after he finished the *Autobiography,* Trollope reasserts his conviction of the importance of realism in fiction.[21] Discussing Dickens and Thackeray, he dismisses the idea that excessive realism can make a work sensational, and thus weaken it. He insists that a good novel is both realistic and sensational and that, if it is true, it cannot be "too" sensational.

Nor was Trollope alone in this emphasis. In review after review of the period, writers comment on the relative degree of realism they find in what they have read. E. S. Dallas, generally regarded as one of the most perceptive of the nineteenth century literary critics, notes in his review of *Rachel Ray* that novels are very like gossip, with the social and moral advantages that novels are respectable. Echoing this thought is the comment of the anonymous reviewer of the same novel for the *Westminster Review,* who says flatly that the reader can "see his neighbor's follies and weaknesses . . . without any tinge of malice" in fiction. The analogy to gossip seems an apt one, as many reviewers do note the way an author deals with private conversations and correspondence, and small details of dress, mannerism, and prejudices. These are the very evidences on which gossip depends heavily.

The idea that characters in fiction should be recognizable as friends and neighbors of the readers is frequently reiterated. Occasionally the reviewer insists that he or she knows someone who could easily have served as the model for a character.[22] More often, the attribution is less specific: "We have all known someone like Mr. Slope." John Jeaffreson notes that Trollope's women in particular are "strictly realistic," and praises him for showing them so clearly in their everyday activities.

Both reviews of Trollope's second novel, *The Kellys and the O'Kellys,* remark upon the authentic quality of the Irish characters. Geraldine

Jewsbury, a regular reviewer for the *Athenaeum*, usually comments favorably on Trollope's ability to draw "lively" characters.[23] "No one has ever drawn English families better," is the judgment of the *Saturday Review*. G. H. Lewes notes with approval Trollope's ability to create in *Orley Farm* and other works complex (and thus true-to-life) characters, rather than the simplistic, all-good or all-evil ones frequently found in popular fiction. And E. S. Dallas notes approvingly that in general Trollope avoids "trickery, false sentiment, morbid pictures," all characteristics of inferior and unrealistic fiction which he finds in the greater number of lending-library novels.

A large part of the realism of characters, for these reviewers, lies in their empathetic quality. Often in the same sentence, a reviewer will note that a character is realistic and elicits sympathy from the reader. William Dixon says of *Orley Farm* that "it is no small triumph for an artist to engage our interests in the heart affairs of an old man of seventy and a woman past forty."[24] Several other reviewers note that characters one would not expect to be appealing, are presented sympathetically — the old, as mentioned above, and the less than virtuous, such as Mr. Scatchard, Alaric Tudor, or Augustus Melmotte. The *North British Review* writer expresses some amazement that Trollope can make the reader feel sorry for the guilty Lady Mason of *Orley Farm*. Dallas remarks that one of the good effects a novel has is to extend the range of the readers' sensibilities, and that Trollope's fiction excels in this area. It is notable that Trollope is commended for the believability and sympathetic quality not only of the morally flawed characters, but also of those who might well be regarded as silly, as for example, Lady Carbury of *The Way We Live Now*.[25] The *Saturday Review* writer notes that the heroic Phineas Finn is made more heroic by reason of his nervous breakdown following the trial in *Phineas Redux*; the collapse makes him both more sympathetic and more believable. In a review of *An Old Man's Love*, published after Trollope's death, Julia Wedgwood notes that in general Thackeray invited his readers to scorn his characters, while the kindly Trollope always urged compassion for his fictive people.

Conversely, when Trollope's novels are criticized, it is often on the grounds of lack of realism. The Newsomes of *Ralph the Heir* are described as not living and moving, according to one review;[26] in another, the novel is not admired because it is too like an exhibit of costumes rather than a picture of living people. Henry James, talking of *Miss MacKenzie*, criticizes the novel as not "true to nature." One reviewer objects strongly to what he perceives as the untruth of the title of *The Way We Live Now*, insisting that he and his friends certainly do not live this way.[27]

Scarcely any of the reviewers object to realism as such, but the writer for the *Saturday Review* notice of *Rachel Ray* feels "there is a vanity and a weariness even in truth of minute descriptions," and expresses the wish that fiction in general "would do something for us besides giving us these accurate likenesses," although that is what is in favor. He acknowledges that his is not a widely-held view, and in fact it was not.

It seems from an overview of the reviews, however, that realism as a characteristic of fiction wanes in importance as the century advances; several of the early novels of Trollope were described as being saved from dullness or mediocrity – or worse – by the realism of characters and incidents. From the seventies on, however, realism is noted, and often praised; but the reviews are as a whole less enthusiastic about the redemptive qualities of that feature alone. The charges of repetitiousness, or of catering to public fancy in choosing plot ideas, are more insistent. Of *Marian Fay*, for example, a reviewer comments that Trollope has shoved a number of currently popular topics together, but not dealt adequately with them.[28] Another notes of this novel that the few admittedly "lively scenes" do not redeem the book. In its obituary notice, the *Times* describes Trollope's works as "each very much the same throughout." The *Saturday Review* notes of *Mr. Scarborough's Family* that, although some of the scenes are good, the story is not original, and the book is flawed by repetition. The *Westminster Review*, given to longer reviews of the early works, devotes only one paragraph to this novel; while not negative, the review is not enthusiastic. This is not to say that all of the later books are reviewed negatively, but only to note that the evidence of a change in public taste toward the more exciting and exotic is growing. Because realism was so essential a part of Trollope's fiction, as the public found that quality less interesting than it had they found Trollope's works less appealing. The metaphor of the photographer, once used as a term of praise for Trollope, now became a disparaging label. Wilde, Haggard, Collins, and Kipling were the writers who displaced Trollope in the public's favor; they wrote about different things, for a different public from the one that Trollope had interested and entertained.

This change in reading taste also accounts in large part for the lack of "staying power" of Trollope's novels after his death in 1882. Of the contemporaries with whom he had shared — and competed for — readers earlier, Dickens and Thackeray continued to be published — frequently in new editions — and listed in literary columns as "gift suggestions" until the end of the century, while no new edition of Trollope's novels was undertaken until 1905. It is not difficult to understand how Thackeray and Dickens, with their richness of exaggeration, survived the vagaries of book-buying tastes more successfully than did Trollope, whom it became fashionable to regard as a drudge rather than a creative artist.

While no other critical issues seem of such commonly-accepted importance to Victorian reviewers as those of the morality and reality of a work, there are several other recurring motifs in the notices of Trollope's novels. One of these is the issue of plot; whether a given novel has a plot or not is often discussed. E. M. Forster's understanding of plot as a story with internal connections between events seems vaguely to be at the foundation of Victorian reviewers' comments. A number of reviews declare a novel to have no plot and proceed to outline the "story" of the work. But the term "plot" is never explicitly defined. Another curious feature of "Plot" comments is that some reviewers find the absence of plot a virtue,[29] while others decry it as a serious failing.[30]

The speed with which Trollope produced his works — both fiction and non-fiction — is another subject for frequent comment. Sometimes the speed itself or the frequency of his publications is noted, usually disparagingly, with the suggestion that he write less often in the future.[31] More often, the style of a work is described as "rushed" or "hastily written," when the criticism is made. A number of reviewers object to the writing of serials on the grounds that such a method of production militates against coherence.[31] Not infrequently the travel books are cited as having been written "as he went along," rather than composed as complete entities at the end of the trip. The result, some reviewers complain, is the repetitiousness and lack of unity characteristic of serialized work.[32]

Vitually every review of the *Autobiography* is positive, and all take note of Trollope's own discussion of his method of composition, and his comparison of a writer's work to that of a cobbler. The *Times* reviewer dismisses his assertions as over-modesty on Trollope's part. He insists that Trollope's work is indeed imaginative and not merely the product of diligent but uninspired labor. The *Athenaeum,* with the *Saturday Review* and *Blackwood's* all have reviews which praise his comments on literature and its composition as sound or having "good sense." The Morleys quite openly agree with Trollope's statement that diligence is more important to success in literature than is inspiration. In later accounts, however, both James Payn and Stephen Gwynn attribute much of Trollope's rather sudden decline in popularity to his own description of his theory and methods of writing fiction.[33]

Trollope's treatment and understanding of women characters comes in for a great deal of comment throughout the reviews. There is a wide divergence of opinion on whether he describes them deeply enough or in too much detail, or defends them excessively or is too severe with them.

Trollope's treatments of clergy and of lawyers are the subject of a fair number of reviewers. Generally, British reviewers praise Trollope's treatment of the clergy, while Irish writers find the clerics less than holy men, and wonder that Trollope does not criticize them more harshly. The majority of those who discuss the lawyers in the novels think that Trollope judges the entire profession too severely.

There is almost no comment at all in any of these reviews on the narrator's role in the novels, although that is one of the paramount concerns of twentieth century readers of Trollope. It is a significant measure of the man and his works, however, that modern scholars find him as interesting a subject as did the readers and reviewers of more than a century ago. And, whatever their judgments about an individual work or its features, there can be no question but that his contemporaries did find Trollope and his works interesting.

Arrangement of the Bibliography

The body of this bibliography has two sections; the first, summarizing articles written about Trollope's works in the fifty-three periodicals surveyed, contains 302 entries. These are arranged in chronological order, and are numbered accordingly. Attribution of authorship of unsigned articles is as given by the *Wellesley Index* and by David Skilton.[34] The second section consists of annotations of articles written by Trollope for the same journals, during the same period. His serialized fiction is not included in this list. The items in this section are numbered with the prefix T, and are likewise arranged chronologically.

The Appendix has five parts. *A* contains a list of journals surveyed. *B* contains a list of entries by the works mentioned in them; *C* is a topic index. *D* and *E* list entries by their authors and publications, respectively.

NOTES

    1.   M. L. Irwin, *Anthony Trollope: A Bibliography* (New York: H. W. Wilson Company, 1925), p. 5
    2.   Michael Sadleir, *Trollope: A Bibliography* (London: Constable, 1928; reprinted London: Dawson's, 1964).
    3.   London: J. Lane, 1913.
    4.   New York: Garland, 1978.
    5.   Port Washington, New York: Kennikat, 1967.
    6.   Helling, p. 7.
    7.   New York: Barnes & Noble, 1969.
    8.   Walter Houghton, ed., Toronto: University of Toronto Press, 1966.
    9.   Houghton, I, xvi.
    10.   London: Longman, 1972.
    11.   A list of the periodicals surveyed for this work appears as Appendix A.
    12,   Skilton, pp. 6-62.
    13.   See below Entry 81.
    14.   See below, Entry 92.
    15.   See below, Entry 94.
    16.   Trollope's views on this subject though doubtless widespread do not accord with the first-hand accounts given to Dr. William Acton as reported by Steven Marcus in *The Other Victorians* (New York: Basic Books, 1964). See especially the first chapter.

17. For a much fuller discussion of this sense of living in transition, see Walter Houghton's *The Victorian Frame of Mind* (New Haven: Yale University, 1975), chapter 1.
13. See G. S. Haight's edition of *The George Eliot Letters* (New Haven: Yale University Press, 1955).
19. Anthony Trollope, *An Autobiography* (Edinburgh and London: William Blackwood, 1883), pp. 122-123.
20. p. 123.
21. See below, Entry T63.
22. See, for example, the *Saturday Review*'s treatment of *Framley Parsonage* (Entry 29 below).
23. Notice her remarks in Entries 12, 15, and 76.
24. Entry 40.
25. See Entries 136 and 137.
26. See Entry 111.
27. See Entry 136.
28. See Entry 219.
29. See below, Entries 88 and 127.
30. See below, Entry 94.
31. See below, Entry 29.
32. Entries 35 and 124.
33. Entries 289 and 301.
34. In his *Anthony Trollope and His Contemporaries* (London: Longman, 1972).

Articles About Trollope

1. [Chorley, Henry F.] "Reviews," *Athenaeum*, no. 1020 (15 May, 1847), 517.

   Review of *The MacDermots of Ballycloran*. This brief notice is devoted chiefly to the difficulties of being the son of a famous writer. Chorley notes with favor that Trollope "seems to possess a vein of humour," but needs a different setting to show it to advantage.

2. [Chorley, Henry F.] "Reviews," *Athenaeum* no. 1081 (15 July, 1848), 701.

   Review of *The Kellys and the O'Kellys*. Chorley "like[s] this novel better than Mr. Trollope's former one," and notes that it is "less painful" than the first. He especially praises the humour and the authentic Irish characters. Trollope here reminds him of Jane Austen, in the ability to create characters.

3. Unsigned. "The Kellys and the O'Kelleys," London *Times* (7 September, 1848), p. 4.

   This review seems less negative than Trollope remembers it in his *Autobiography*. It praises the "native humour" and "bold reality" of characterization, and terms the work both "substantial" and "very corse."

4. Unsigned. "Literary Notices," *New Monthly Magazine*, 83 (1848), 544-545.

   Review of *The Kellys and the O'Kellys*. Commenting that this novel is a "well-told and intensely Irish tale," the reviewer describes

Irish people as wild and whimsical. He sketches the plot, noting that "Mr. Trollope does not spare Irishmen of any rank or creed," and suggests that the novel's success lies largely in the fact that the characters fully deserve the sad fates which await them at the conclusion.

5. [Jewsbury, Geraldine.] "Reviews," *Athenaeum*, no. 1422 (27 January 1855), 107-108.

Review of *The Warden*. Jewsbury characterizes the novel as "a clever, spirited, sketchy story," which is marred only by "too much indifference as to the rights of the case" of the wardenship and salary; this indifference is held responsible for the "very lame and unsatisfactory conclusion." She summarizes the plot and quotes at some length a dialogue between Archdeacon Grantly and his wife.

6. [St. John, H., or Chorley, Henry F.] "Reviews," *Athenaeum*, no. 1544 (30 May, 1857), 689-690.

Review of *Barchester Towers*. The reviewer comments on the difficulty of writing successful sequels, and judges this one is even better than its predecessor: "it is certainly more dramatic . . . , the characters are more varied; an infusion of romance gives lightness" to the clerical setting. He wryly recounts Mr. Slope's fall, noting that Trollope seems to enjoy satirizing anything associated with the "Low Church." He notes that although the book "is ecclesiastical in its interest," it will be enjoyed by a wider audience than churchmen.

7. Unsigned. "Reviews," *Saturday Review*, 3 (30 May, 1857), 503-504.

Review of *Barchester Towers*. This unidentified reviewer finds the book "if anything, too clever," and proceeds to outline the plot. He praises it as having "more power and finish" than *The*

Warden. He likes Trollope's handling of the central conflict, and the clergymen: "He sees and paints the follies of either extreme." The only flaw found is the "disjointed" nature of the story.

8. [Dallas, E. S.] "New Novels," London *Times* (13 August, 1857), p. 5.

   Review of *Barchester Towers*. Dallas begins with a critical discussion of recent novels in general, finding them to be poorly disguised sermons, heavy and serious in tone, or over-flowery, weak imitations of Dickens. He finds *Barchester Towers* to be refreshingly different from the bulk of current fiction. The author is praised for his handling of clergy, who are too often portrayed as "either ridiculous or utterly insipid" by other writers. He offers a synopsis of the plot, noting especially the characterization. Mr. Grantly is praised as the "clerical ideal, good, sober . . . , moderate in opinion and exceedingly correct in all social observances." The flaws of the novel are, Dallas says, an occasional "tediousness of explanation" and a rather uninformed and unfair picture of newspapers. No doubt the last observation was inspired by the satiric attacks on the *Jupiter,* which most read as a thinly disguised London *Times.*

9. [Meredith, George.] "Contemporary Literature: Belles Lettres," *Westminster Review,* 68 (October, 1857), 326-327.

   Review of *Barchester Towers*. Meredith praises this work as "decidedly the cleverest novel of the season, and one of the most masculine delineations of modern life in a special class of society . . . ." He adds that the reader, while sure of an eventually happy outcome, can still enjoy worrying about the characters as the plot proceeds. The characters are praised as true: "We have all met someone like Mr. Slope." Trollope is mildly criticized for being "too sketchy" and for not swaying the reader's emotions very much, although for the most part he is to be admired as a "caustic and vigorous" writer.

10. [Maine, Henry.] "Reviews," *Saturday Review*, 4 (5 December, 1857), 517-518.

Review of *The Three Clerks*. Maine calls the new novel by Trollope very "smart" and full of promise as well as faults. The major flaw found is evidence of haste in writing. The characterization is almost comparable to Thackeray's; Trollope's mastery of such a range — from Katie Woodward to the "rougher types" in the Civil Service — is remarkable.

11. [Jewsbury, Geraldine.] "Reviews," *Athenaeum*, no. 1574 (26 December, 1857), 1621.

Review of *The Three Clerks*. Jewsbury praises Trollope's new novel as having "more of story, with stronger individual interest" than the two Barchester novels. She sketches the plot, wonders whether the audience should be led to sympathize so much with Alaric Tudor, but finds the punishment fully adequate. Although the satire is faulted as "not so finished as in *The Warden*," Jewsbury thinks it may be a more popular novel.

12. [Jewsbury, Geraldine.] "Reviews," *Athenaeum*, no. 1597 (5 June, 1858), 719.

Review of *Dr. Thorne*. On the grounds of "genuine humour" and outstanding characterization, Jewsbury finds this an excellent book. She comments chiefly on the various characters, remarking on Trollope's ability to bare their weaknesses and yet not condemn them. Sir Roger Scatchard's story "moves to a pity deeper than tears." She concludes by observing that the only fault is the excessive length (one third of the novel could be omitted), yet she strongly recommends it.

13. [Maine, Henry.] "Reviews," *The Saturday Review*, 5 (12 June, 1858), 618-619.

Review of *Dr. Thorne*. Maine feels that there is evidence of a falling-off of Trollope's powers here, and blames it on Trollope's rapidity of novel production. The characterization he finds good, but notes that with care it could have been much better; the story is "slight," but has possibilities not realized here. He chides Trollope for apologizing for possible legal errors rather than verifying points before writing the story. He attacks Trollope's suggestion that love ought always be gratified and that honesty will be financially rewarded.

14. [Capes, J. M.] "Literary Notices," *The Rambler: A Catholic Journal and Review*, n.s., 10 (August, 1858), 142-143.

Review of *Dr. Thorne*. Reviewer Capes expresses thanks that there are some good novels (i.e., with wholesome moral values extolled) being produced. He considers Trollope's past works, finding both *The Warden* and *Barchester Towers* to be first rate, but *The Three Clerks* is judged a failure. *Dr. Thorne* is a piece of "shrewd, sensible, vivacious fiction," Cape feels. Overall, he predicts that Trollope will "run to seed before his summertime has fairly begun," and burn out as a writer of good novels.

15. [Jewsbury, Geraldine.] "Reviews," *Athenaeum*, no. 1639 (26 March, 1859), 420.

Review of *The Bertrams*. Jewsbury begins with rather faint praise for this novel – it will "keep up the author's reputation." She complains that the story is too long, no doubt padded to fill the customary three volumes. Too much of the plot is set in the Orient, which is too far from England. The characters, however, she finds lively and "boldly-drawn;" they compensate for the novel's obvious faults. All in all, however, she thinks readers will find *The Bertrams* "deeply interesting."

16. Unsigned. "Reviews," *Saturday Review*, 7 (26 March, 1859), 368-369.

Review of *The Bertrams*. The reviewer speaks of Trollope's work in general as always attaining the primary end of novels, "pleasure and amusement." Trollope, he says, writes as a gentleman, being both very observant and very kindly. *The Bertrams* is described as the most enjoyable of Trollope's novels to date, as it has a more clearly defined plot than the earlier, sketchier stories. The argument of this novel, which he sees as a defense of "love in a cottage," is not, however, always validly made. The novel is flawed in minor ways by unnecessary tangents and the interweaving of actual people and events into the story; these manipulations make the plot literally impossible. The novel would be better if Trollope would either omit serious issues, such as matters of religious dogma, or else deal with them more adequately; he often introduces them as topics of conversation, only to drop or dismiss them as finally inconsequential.

17. Unsigned. "Literature of the Month," *New Monthly Magazine*, 115 (April, 1859), 497-500.

Review of *The Bertrams*. This is a brief one-paragraph notice of the novel. The reviewer sketches the plot and describes it as "a rattling, social novel, full of character and replete with incident and scenery." He comments that in this, as many other contemporary novels, the expansion of railway travel has clearly affected the setting of the story.

18. [Dallas, E. S.] "Anthony Trollope," London *Times*, 23 May, 1859, p. 12.

Dallas discusses at some length the influence of Mudie's lending library on both the reading public and the authors of novels. He calls Trollope the "most fertile, the most popular, the most successful author . . . of the circulating library sort," and finds Trollope free from the faults of most circulating library novelists — namely, "Trickery, false sentiment, morbid pictures." Trollope's novels are wholesome and honest, though perhaps sometimes too predictable. In *The Warden,* Dallas sees the Archdeacon as the most successfully drawn character; he finds Mr. Harding to be "all goodness and meekness, soft and gelatinous." He mentions that *Barchester Towers* has earlier been praised in the *Times. The Three Clerks* he praises briefly as "a brilliant tale" and better than some of Dickens' over-caricatured works. *Dr. Thorne* and *The Bertrams,* he feels, are less distinctive but no less interesting. He notes that Trollope puts the readers in possession of "the secrets of all hearts" and lets them "see the inevitable sequence of events"; this narrative method can lead to boredom with the foolishness of a character's actions. But all of these novels, he asserts, are the work of a good and thoughtful man.

19. [Roscoe, W. C.] "The Bertrams, *National Review,* 9 (July, 1859), 187-199.

"This novel is inferior to Mr. Trollope's previous works," is the opening remark of this reviewer. Roscoe regrets the lack of satire and of "bonhomie" in *The Bertrams.* Taken by itself, however, this novel is not a bad one; and that fact, Roscoe feels, is surprising as this is the fifth Trollope novel in a relatively short time. Trollope is here adjudged better at "matters of sentiment" than either George Eliot or William Thackeray; in matters of thought and opinion Trollope is disappointing. Roscoe criticizes Trollope for his negative treatment of lawyers and his treatment of George Bertram's translation of scriptures.

20. Unsigned. "Trollope's West Indies." *Saturday Review,* 8 (26 November, 1859), 643-645.

Review of *The West Indies and the Spanish Main.* Although this reviewer thinks the West Indies a "forlorn and insipid part of the civilized world," he admits that "Mr. Trollope has shown himself equal to the task of making the narrative . . . very amusing and very interesting." The amusement comes, he continues, not from "galvanized jokes" but from "clear, racy, vigorous descriptions of men and things" which Trollope encountered. Trollope does not, he feels, make the reader want to go to the West Indies, but he tells fully what everyone ought to know about it. He summarizes the treatment of Jamaica, noting that it refutes the English romanticized picture of the "nigger" with facts and with sympathy for the black man's plight. He discusses the race and class problems Trollope found, and reiterates the value of this work for British people.

21. —. "Mr. Trollope on Central America," *Saturday Review,* 8 (3 December, 1859), 675-676.

Second part of 2-part review of *The West Indies and the Spanish Main.* The reviewer notes that Trollope found New Granada and Costa Rica even more desolate and barbarous than Jamaica. He summarizes the itinerary and praises Trollope's lively mind and his willingness to put up with the difficulties of the trip. This book has, the reviewer feels, the first clear account of the problems connected with crossing the isthmus of Panama.

22. Unsigned. "Contemporary Literature," *Westminster Review,* 73, o.s. (January, 1860), 163.

Review of *The West Indies and the Spanish Main.* This reviewer cites Trollope as having a "clever, lively, sensible manner." He remarks on the vast amount of first-hand knowledge of the peoples, the government, and the area which are contained in the book, and briefly summarizes Trollope's opinions on the political, economic, and racial problems of this part of the world.

23. [Dallas, E. S.] "West Indies and the Spanish Main," London *Times,* 6 January, 1860, p. 4.

In this quite lengthy first part of a two-part review, Dallas has high praise for Tollope's work. He claims that by amusing the readers with accounts of his many adventures and mishaps,

Trollope has "inveigled" them into learning about an important part of the world. The people and customs are well described, he feels. He summarizes at length Trollope's views of the natives as lazy and dependent and very impulsive, but loyal as pets to their white masters. Trollope vigorously defends the plantation owners, and cites many cases of their generosity towards the natives. The reviewer agrees with Trollope that one solution to the labor problem is the importing of coolies from the Orient; these are workers who will work. He also agrees with Trollope that the existence in the Jamaican Parliament of black natives largely explains that government's widespread corruption. He blames the emancipation of the blacks for most of the social problems, citing their primitive habits and uneducated dialect. The French are praised for their more successful colonization methods.

24. —. "Trollope's Travels," London *Times*, 18 January, 1860, p. 12.

This review is a continuation of the preceding one. Here Dallas focusses on travel and transportation, especially in Panama. He summarizes Trollope's experiences and his research into the proposals for a canal across Panama and the problems which the current proposals have not yet solved. He describes the present procedure of transferring passengers and freight from ship to railroad to ship to cross Panama. Dallas concludes that this part of Trollope's work is not so interesting nor so carefully written as that part dealing with the peoples.

25. [Jewsbury, Geraldine]. "Reviews," *Athenaeum* no. 1699 (19 May, 1860), 681.

Review of *Castle Richmond*. Jewsbury praises the story here, while disliking the characters; this is a virtual reversal of her usual Trollope stance. She feels Trollope is too hard upon Owen, and has created a detestable monster in the Countess of Desmond. She recommends the work "to persons in search of a good, well-written novel, with plenty of genuine sense and interest in it."

26. Unsigned. "Reviews," *Saturday Review,* 9 (19 May, 1860), 643-644.

Review of *Castle Richmond.* This is a rather mixed review, by a person who says he or she usually admires Trollope's fiction. Trollope has chosen a significant background for the story — the Irish famine — but should have written more directly about it. The reviewer calls this a "commonform story," only marred by the introduction of a rivalry between mother and daughter. He takes strong exception to this unsavory situation. Admitting that Trollope doubtless has difficulties thinking up new yet conventional women characters and incidents, he nonetheless thinks that here Trollope has committed an "artistic impropriety." He chides the author for encouraging young people to marry for love without regard to security; this sort of writing only encourages an already widespread and imprudent tendency. Although the novel is, on the whole, clever and amusing, Trollope should not treat theological matters so lightly and should transcribe dialect more carefully or not at all.

27. Unsigned. "Contemporary Literature: Belles Lettres," *Westminster Review,* 74 (October, 1860), 312.

Review of *Castle Richmond.* This reviewer praises the novel as "very interesting . . . not easy to lay . . . aside." He summarizes the plot and remarks on Trollope's skill and clarity of characterization and his naturalness of narration: there is "no mechanical art in the gradual unfolding" of the plot, no artificial suspense.

28. Unsigned. "Reviews," *Athenaeum* no. 1741 (9 March, 1861), 319-320.

Review of *Orley Farm*. This reviewer has high praise for Trollope's fiction, particularly because of the characters who seem like "living personal friends" to readers. The first part of *Orley Farm*, just published, promises well for the rest, he feels. He quotes at length from the novel's presentation of the major characters and incorrectly predicts the reappearance of the Barchester characters in the latter part of the novel.

29. Unsigned. "Reviews," *Saturday Review*, 9 (4 May, 1861), 451-452.

Review of *Framley Parsonage*. Opening with remarks on the immense popularity of Trollope's novels, this reviewer likens the characters to the neighbors of the readers. Thackeray has written of the same class, he finds, and has written more deeply about them, especially in *Vanity Fair*. *Framley Parsonage* he feels is less brillinat than *Barchester Towers*; it seems that as Trollope "becomes more successful, he becomes more tame." He fears that the author "may at last degenerate into a mere raconteur, whose monthly mission is to gossip." This reviewer dislikes the practice of "borrowing" characters from previous novels, as the readers will lose interest in them unless their interiors are shown more clearly. Trollope makes a good dinner table companion, this reviewer feels, as he excels at exaggeration and caricature. Here, however, he finds the plot weak, the conclusion too abrupt; these flaws may be due to serialization, which is very bad for writers. He hopes that Trollope's next work will have a new plot, new characters.

30. Unsigned. "Contemporary Literature: Belles Lettres," *Westminster Review*, 76 (July, 1861), 152-153.

Review of *Framley Parsonage*. This reviewer is harshly critical of the novel. It is termed "trivial" and "purposeless," flawed by a "glibness of composition." Part of the fault lies, he feels, in the fact that the novel was written for serialization; such a manner of publication usually destroys coherence. The reviewer gives a brief account of the plot, criticizing the use of characters from other novels and the Trollope habit of portraying clergymen in an unfavorable light. The reviewer concludes that there is no plot development here, simply an "aggregation" of events.

31. Unsigned. "Tales of All Countries," *Saturday Review*, 12 (7 December, 1861), 587-588.

"Mr. Trollope is alone in his ability to make a story about absolutely nothing," is the judgement of this critic. He notes that the stories are wonders of composition, and, for people who like this sort of writing, the volume will not be disappointing. After describing briefly the substance of several of the stories, he concludes that noen of them approach the quality of the novels.

32. Donnelly, Thomas. "Modern Periodical Literature," *Dublin Review*, 51 (May, 1862), 275-308.

Mr. Donnelly devotes this article to a criticism of the wide range of popular magazines; his remarks are generally negative. Of *Temple Bar*, now edited by Anthony Trollope, he says that it has "no distinctive character," and groups it with other magazines, such as *Household Words*, *Cornhill* and *Macmillan's*, as having too much light literature and too little information in the articles on such topics as politics.

33. Unsigned. "Reviews," *Athenaeum*, no. 1804 (24 May, 1862), 685-687.

Review of *North America*. After commenting that the Trollope family seems to owe the United States something after Mrs. Trollope's "clever and spiteful" picture of life there, the reviewer notes that this book may even the score. He praises the tone of Anthony Trollope's book as the work of a "good old traveller."

He quotes several passages from the work and comments on the spoiling of American children by their parents and on the pallor of Americans caused by central hot-air heating, one of the many mechanical systems Americans seem too engrossed in.

34. Unsigned. "Trollope's North America," *Saturday Review*, 13 (31 May, 1862), 625-626.

This reviewer finds the work "sensible enough, and moderate, and written in the spirit and style of a gentleman. But it is most terribly windbaggy." He notes that all readers are familiar with the standard tour of the United States, and Trollope is merely giving us another one. Trollope could have said all the worthwhile things in 100 pages, and omitted the other 800 pages of this work. Among the few new things discussed in this book is "the intense disagreeableness of the ordinary American woman," caused by a misunderstanding of the nature of chivalry. Also, the unpleasant rudeness of the "common Yankee" is accounted for by the very real belief of Americans in the equality of all men. He notes that Trollope also points out that Americans are, as a group, very respectful of government and the laws, and they trust their elected officials to manage things. He objects to the lengthy treatment of the Civil War here, as he feels that Trollope has nothing to contribute on this topic.

35. Unsigned. "North America by Anthony Trollope," *London Times*, 11 June, 1862, p. 6.

The reviewer commends Trollope's powers of observation and his treatment of major American events, such as the Civil War, as well as minor, everyday occurrences. He cites Trollope's treatment of the Fremont affair as new and illuminating for British readers. He comments on the Civil War, the high literacy rate, the dishonesty of employers, the corruption of some politicians, and America's distrust of England. He defends the right of English writers to criticize the U. S. The only fault he finds with

with this work is the apparent haste with which it was written and the resulting flaws in organization.

36. Unsigned. "North America (by Anthony Trollope)." *Fraser's Magazine,* 66 (July, 1862), 256-264.

This review begins by noting several flaws the writer finds in this work — chiefly, its wordiness. He proceeds to discuss sections of the book. Most of the review is devoted to political corruption and the Civil War. He notes several points of difference between himself and Trollope on the nature of the antipathy between North and South, and concludes that what the United States needs most is humility.

37. Unsigned. "Trollope's America," *Dublin University Magazine,* 60 (July 1862), 75-82.

This reviewer does not seem well acquainted with some of the issues here; he begins by noting that Anthony Trollope must be very proud of his mother's earlier work on North America. He also commends Mrs. Trollope's book as having been very efficacious in improving the manners of the Americans (without offering any evidence that this is so). This work is cited as having "a very full account of the Northern and Western States." (Trollope did not travel west of St. Louis, Missouri.) The reviewer finds Trollope too severe on the South, and imprudent in defending the U. S. national debt. He gives a synopsis of the topics covered in the work and includes several quotations. There is no mention in this review of tone or style; it discusses content exclusively.

38. Unsigned. "The War in America," *New Monthly Magazine,* 125 (July, 1862), 343-353.

This writer considers a number of books and articles about the American Civil War, including Trollope's *North America.* He cites Trollope's book here primarily as an authority on the war, rather than as the subject of a review. The writer finds evidence to support his own views that the Americans apparently intend to annex Canada as a step toward their goal of conquering the world; this intention is a primary cause for the United States' hostility to England.

39. Hamley, Edward B. "Trollope's North America," *Blackwood's Edinburgh Magazine,* 42 (September, 1862), 372-390.

Hamley commends Trollope's style as "brisk and flowing," having an air of confidence; he notes that he also enjoyed the book on the Spanish Main because of its "light, sparkling, and agreeable" tone. The timing of this work, Hamley feels, is not quite the best, as the Civil War is still in progress. He finds fault with Trollope's pro-North position, which may be the cause of the author's not answering adequately the questions Great Britain asks about the war. Hamley defends stoutly and at length the right of any party to secede from an agreement which is no longer satisfactory. Hamley suggests that Trollope should write more novels and stop attempting political analyses.

40. [Dixon, William H.] "Reviews," *Athenaeum,* no. 1823 (4 October, 1862), 425-426.

Review of *Orley Farm.* Dixon begins by noting that this is not about Barchester and that "it is not a pleasant book." He outlines the plot, quoting an extensive passage relating Sir Peregrine's thoughts about Lady Mason, and concludes that "it is no small triumph for an artist to engage our interests in heart affairs of an old man of seventy and a woman past forty."

41. Unsigned. "Reviews," *Saturday Review,* 14 (11 October 1862), 444-445. Review of *Orley Farm.*

Review of *Orley Farm.* This reviewer praises the novel as pleasing and amusing (the proper ends of novels he believes), from beginning to end. He notes approvingly the "new" setting and plot for Trollope. "No one has ever drawn English families better," he comments, and continues, "how hard it is to sketch such [ordinary] persons in a story may be guessed by the fact that hardly any novelists have succeeded in it." Lady Mason is superbly done, he asserts. Trollope is, however, very unfair to the legal system and to lawyers in general, he finds.

42. [Lewes, G. H., prob.] "Our Survey of Literature," *Cornhill Magazine,* 6 (November, 1862), 702.

Review of *Orley Farm.* After opening with the high praise that this is "in some respects the finest of Mr. Anthony Trollope's works," and that it will make readers "better for the rest of their days," Lewes quickly moves to consider the novel's faults. The novel is, he asserts, "badly constructed," contains unnecessary scenes, and presents a number of characters who are "very far from successful." On the whole, however, his attitude is one of "grateful admiration" for the work. He proceeds to discuss the popular demand for believable characters who are also simplistic, and priases Trollope at length for the complexity of his characters, and their ability to elicit sympathy from the reader even in their imperfection. Trollope, he feels, teaches true charity through his novels.

43. Unsigned. "Orley Farm." London *Times,* 26 December, 1862, p. 5.

The reviewer remarks on the large number of recent novels involving legal disputes, and declares *Orley Farm* to be equal to any other. He summarizes the story at some length and praises Trollope for his subtlety and complexity of characterization, and his handling of passion.

44. [Cunningham, Henry S.] "Orley Farm," *National Review,* 16 (January, 1863), 27-40.

Cunningham opens by referring to a recent article in a French journal which is critical of British fiction and its "boasted prudery," especially in the light of some recent real-life British scandals. Cunningham then notes that *Orley Farm* is an adequate answer to the French charges, as the novel expresses "the precise standard of English taste, sentiment, and conviction." Every well-informed British person, he continues, is quite familiar with a great number of Trollope's characters, and general conversation about them is as frequent as it is about art exhibits and international news. The only justifiable complaint about Trollope's work is that he cannot produce a tragedy; there are many good things in his writing that more than offset this complaint.

45. Unsigned. "Trollope's Novels," *North British Review*, 38 (February, 1863), 185-188.

The reviewer begins with general praise of Trollope as an author who writes "rapidly and with gusto;" although he lacks the ability to deal with psychological insight or with great passion, he is genial and observant and "quite satisfactory." Trollope's popular success, the reviewer feels, is due to his unflagging spirit and his good sense; in the future, these novels will have a "certain historical value." *Orley Farm* is the best of the novels, he feels, although it contains too many characters and incidents. The reviewer finds it amazing that Trollope can win sympathy for a woman so clearly guilty.

46. Unsigned. "Trollope's Tales of All Countries, 2nd series," *Saturday Review*, 15 (28 February, 1863), 276-278.

This collection is compared to the sketches which a painter might make casually, intending either to work on or to dismiss later. The reviewer outlines several of the stories and disparages them with the exception of the conclusion of "A Ride Across Palestine," which he finds to be superior.

47. Unsigned. "Modern Novel and Romance," *Dublin University Magazine,* 61 (April, 1863), 436-442.

This writer divides current novels into three classes: the enigma (e.g., Wilkie Collins' works), the class novel (e.g., Trollope's novels), and the sensational novel (e.g., Mrs. Woods' *East Lynne*). About Trollope, the reviewer says that the novelist "photographs the clerical exterior, but does not go below the surface." He claims that Trollope is unsurpassed at noticing and describing the clerical class, and the "unholy class" pictured in *Orley Farm.* The essay then proceeds to a discussion of the decline in public morality, and expresses regret that prominent people are seen publicly with their mistresses, and are commonly known to have other vices, to the extent that such things are now a matter of popular conversation. One cannot fairly object to the reflection of this reality in fiction, but one must regret that it occurs.

48. [Jeaffreson, John C.] "Reviews," *Athenaeum,* no. 1877 (17 October, 1863), 492-494.

Review of *Rachel Ray.* This is a very lengthy review, and very positive. The novel, it asserts, will help "to correct existing vices of public taste" ([i.e., for sensational novels]. Jeaffreson praises Trollope's ability to portray women, especially women in their everyday postures and activities. He describes the novel as "strictly realistic," noted for its spirit of "merry lightness of heart and unaffected gaiety."

49. Unsigned. "Reviews," *Saturday Review,* 16 (24 October, 1863), 554-555.

Review of *Rachel Ray.* This writer begins by noting that Trollope is a master of drawing young women who are "very like real young women, and yet distinct, ingenuous, and interesting." He gives an account of the plot of the novel, and comments that Trollope loves to depict vulgar and shabby-genteel people as well as clergymen. Trollope succeeds rather well, the reviewer thinks, especially with the Tappit family and Mr. Prong. Trollope is comparable to Miss Yonge and to Thackeray. The only objection this reviewer has is that "there is a vanity and a weariness even in truth of minute descriptions." He finds that one does read and enjoy Trollope's novels, and then finds them lacking. "We wish fiction would do something for us besides giving us these accurate likenesses of those whom we see or know." But, until fiction does change, the reviewer seems to sigh, Trollope is one of the best at producing "the article in demand."

50. [Dalles, E. S.] "New Novels," London *Times*, 25 December, 1863, p. 4.

Review of *Rachel Ray*. Dallas begins by pointing out that novels are very like gossip, with the advantage that one need not be ashamed or embarrassed to participate in the former. Novels serve a good end for the reader by widening the range of one's sympathies and teaching one to care as much for the problems of the common people as those of the "great and mighty." Dallas has high praise for Trollope, who "abjures improbabilities" and shows great judgment in his writing. He compares Trollope with Thackeray and George Eliot; they all have great and sound knowledge of human nature. Trollope understands women better than any other contemporary writer, he says, and Trollope describes both great and small emotions very precisely. In *Rachel Ray,* the only weakness that he finds is an excessive degree of concern with propriety in small matters. He declares it a pleasant novel nonetheless.

51. Unsigned. "Contemporary Literature: Belles Lettres," *Westminster Review*, 81 (January, 1864), 136-138.

Review of *Rachel Ray*. This reviewer has only praise for this novel: "A good design correctly drawn and coloured, though the subject be homely and prosaic." He commends Trollope for allowing the reader "to see his neighbor's follies and weaknesses in a thoroughly ridiculous light, without any tinge of malice." Character delineation here is especially outstanding, the reviewer feels. He includes several lengthy quotations to illustrate his point.

52. [Jeaffreson, John C.] "Reviews," *Athenaeum,* no. 1900 (26 March, 1864), 437-438.

Review of *Small House at Allington.* Jeaffreson comments on the fact that Lily Dale and Johnny Eames have become everyday topics of conversation in the world at large; no one dare not having read this novel. He praises Trollope's handling of Adolphus Crosbie, noting that even his perfidy is fully understood by the reader. The slow development of Crosbie's change is wonderful. Several scenes are described as "clever," although those at the boarding house are disparaged as "vulgar." Jeaffreson considers Eames to be a boring character, and asserts that only old ladies such as Lady Julia de Guest could care much for him. He concludes the review with a "demand" that Trollope write again to tell "the further fortunes of the characters," except for those who live in Burton Crescent.

53. Kinnear, A. S. "Mr. Trollope's Novels," *North British Review,* 40, o.s., 1 n.s. (May, 1864), 193-210.

Kinnear notes that Trollope is not a scholar, but an enjoyer of life, and this fact is the source of the charm of his novels. He praises Trollope's writing as vivacious, graceful, and, chiefly, true. There may occasionally be too many tangential incidents for some tastes — but, Kinnear argues, real life is like that. He discusses at some length the characterization of the clergy, Mrs. Proudie, and the lower-class characters. He insists that the function of novels is to amuse, and not to "disquiet the mind" of the reader. He criticizes Trollope's harsh attitude toward lawyers, and concludes that "no novels are more pleasant than the best of Mr. Trollope's."

Unsigned. "The Small House at Allington," *Saturday Review,* 17 (14 May, 1864), 595-596.

This reviewer begins a favorable review with the judgment that "Mr. Trollope has achieved another great success in his own peculiar line." No one, he asserts, could describe the inner feelings of young people of respectable families any more accurately than does this author. The narration of this novel cannot be praised too highly, he feels, and the character of Crosbie is a masterpiece. He mentions a number of other characters, and notes that he only wishes that Mrs. Dale had told Lily how foolish it is to pine after an unworthy lover. The presentation of Lily may encourage people to think that Trollope agrees with her, which the reviewer doubts. He discusses the issue of whether a novelist ought to have all the elements of a story conclude so as to edify the reader, and notes that Trollope would surely insist that credibility be first observed. The only real flaw here, this reviewer feels, is the inclusion of some unnecessary scenes, including the Dumbello-Palliser set.

[Washburn, W. T.] "The Small House at Allington," *North American Review,* 99 (July, 1864), 292-298.

Review of *The Small House at Allington.* This reviewer calls the novel "a fair picture of English country life," and praises the well-conceived characters and the dash of humor he observes. He notes that Trollope is more the novelist than the philosopher, but is admired by Americans for his honest, if unsuccessful, attempts to portray their country and its institutions accurately. Washburn finds Trollope's chief virtue as a writer in his description of minute details of circumstance and incident, and feels he is a better painter of women characters than is Thackeray, though over-all Thackeray is superior in characterization. Trollope lacks humor, Washburn thinks, because he limits his observations to the surface of things; in this he is most closely comparable to Jane Austen. The reviewer describes several characters in the novel, and criticizes the treatment of Johnny Eames, "whose development stopped at the asinine stage." He notes that a sequel to this story is forthcoming, but concludes that this novel is not lively enough for "an American schoolboy."

56. Unsigned. "Miss Mackenzie," *Saturday Review,* 19 (4 March, 1865), 262-265.

The reviewer comments on Trollope's habit of filling his novels with "nice people;" the only exception to this is *Brown, Jones, and Robinson,* of which novel "it may be questioned whether any living being ever got to the end" of it. *Miss Mackenzie* is certainly not like that, the review states, but it is quite different from Trollope's usual product, as most of the characters are dull and disagreeable. Trollope seems to take money worries very seriously, and does not see them as subjects for comedy; the reviewer notes that Trollope has no Micawbers or Skimpoles here. He admires Trollope's respect and tenderness for those "poets who cannot sing" — people who feel deeply but cannot express themselves well. Nonetheless, the valuable truths which Trollope wants the readers to see here do not, for this reviewer, compensate for the tediousness of arriving at them. He notes some good sketches and scenes, but objects to the stupidly coined names. He concludes that this novel is a "monstrously prosaic version of Mariana in the moated grange."

57. Unsigned. "Miss MacKenzie," *Pall Mall Gazette,* 1 (March, 1865), 7.

This writer notes that Trollope has produced many books, among them only one failure (not here named). He does the difficult task of catching the charm of everyday life very well: "His hero is a tough old cock . . . his heroine a dowdy old hen," yet he manages to awaken our interest in them. The reviewer then sketches the plot, noting Trollope's understanding of his characters' thoughts and fears, and commends his mastery of drawing clerical figures in particular.

58. Unsigned. "Another Cluster of Novels," *Dublin University Magazine*, 65 (May, 1865), 570-581.

This is a review of a large number of recent novels, including one paragraph on *Miss Mackenzie*. The reviewer praises Trollope's ability to make the prosaic life of middle class people appear poetic. He notes especially the minuteness of detail in descriptions of the flaws and idiosyncracies of various characters. However, the reviewer feels, this novel proves that the possibilities of contemptible clergy have been exhausted: "Let lawyers and physicians have a turn again" as the butts of popular novels.

59. Unsigned. "Contemporary Literature: Belles Lettres," *Westminster Review*, 83 (July, 1865), 133-134.

Review of *Miss Mackenzie* and *Can You Forgive Her?* The reviewer begins by commenting that, in the past, many have criticized novels as too likely to "dazzle" young readers with unrealistic pictures of glamour and "delights" they would probably never in fact experience. Now, he goes on, the danger of novel reading is that it may induce a "loathing of all civilized life." Most of the characters in *Miss Mackenzie* are odious; the novel suggests that because the heroine has money, she ought not trust anyone. If a judgment can be made from the first volume of a novel, however, *Can You Forgive Her?* seems to this reviewer to be much more promising. Alice he describes as a young woman "infected with the nineteenth century idea that there was something important for her to do with her life." He similarly finds Glencora an unsympathetic character, but feels that

Trollope has a real appreciation for the complexity of pressures on the modern young person, and has a "tone of moral soundness" which justifies his sympathy for evil-doers. Trollope's principal fault, the review notes, is that he has the same idea too many times.

60. James, Henry. Untitled Review. *Nation,* 1 (13 July, 1865), 51.

Review of *Miss Mackenzie.* James admits that he enjoys reading Trollope but is embarrassed that he does. He summarizes the plot of the novel and notes that the heroine is immature. Trollope may be "true to common life," James says, but it is doubtful whether he is "true to nature." He feels Trollope's characters are barely better than imbeciles. "He has deliberately selected vulgar illustrations," to make matters worse. He thinks that both Trollope and Thackeray lack imagination, but feels Thackeray has judgment where Trollope does not. He asks why Trollope does not "observe great things as well as little ones," since he is a close observer. While Trollope has many of the qualities of a first-rate writer, he is not one because he lacks a larger vision.

61. Stewart, Charles. "Review," *Fortnightly Review,* 1 (1 August 1865), 765-767.

Review of *Hunting Sketches.* Stewart cites the "business-like air" of this book. The tone, he says, shows that the author likes and knows about hunting. He comments that Trollope's novels are more like photographs than pictures, because their observation is so complete. About hunting Trollope has written very precisely in *Orley Farm.* This book, he continues, is an account of "the company to be met at the cover-side" and how they "comport themselves." It is true, sympathetic to the weak, and entertaining, and, the reviewer notes, it defends the propriety of parsons joining in hunts.

62. Unsigned. "Reviews," *Saturday Review*, 20 (19 August, 1865), 240-242.

Review of *Can You Forgive Her?* The reviewer begins by commenting that jilting is not the worst social offense possible, but is certainly a very popular offense to write about. He notes that while Alice Vavasor's jiltings were done from noble motives, especially when compared to Adolphus Crosbie's act, Alice was still in the wrong, though no one would call her a scoundrel. The reviewer notes that men usually jilt women for selfish reasons, and women usually jilt men for unselfish reasons. Alice's problem, he feels, is that she "has let her mind become filled with some notions of the grandeur and importance of making the best of life . . . . What would be the best use she has no sort of idea." Trollope's abilities at characterization are quite obvious in this woman, the reviewer states. He notes that, unlike many authors, Trollope never forgets what he has said about a character, and thus his characters are always consistent. He sees the novel as a statement by Trollope that there is no point in making "too much fuss about any theory of life," as that will get in the way of living a life. He notes that Trollope's many young women readers may not like this theme and its prosaic lesson. He feels that Trollope is perhaps too smug and comfortable in his opinion. However, he notes, the dialogue and letters are wonderfully lifelike. The secondary characters also deserve praise; Burgo Fitzgerald, Mrs. Greenow and her suitor, and Alice's father are all first-rate. Trollope should, he states, get another illustrator; this one's [H. K. Browne] pictures often contradict the verbal descriptions, and are "vulgar," "insipid and weak."

63. Unsigned. "Recent Novels," London *Times*, 23 August, 1865, p. 12.

Review of *Miss Mackenzie* and three other novels. The reviewer comments on the enormous number of novels now on the market, both serially and in complete volumes. He judges *Miss Mackenzie* to be one of Trollope's best if not his most appealing, because this is not his usual romantic material. Actuality is the highest quality of a good novel, the reviewer states, and this novel is about real life; furthermore, Trollope is able, through his skill in narration, to make essentially dull people truly interesting to the reader.

64. James, Henry. Untitled Review. *Nation*, 1 (28 September, 1856), 409.

Review of *Can You Forgive Her?* James has virtually nothing good to say of this novel or its author. He asserts that Trollope has one style and that merely by changing some characters' names, one novel becomes identical with another. He outlines the three plots of this work, noting that they are all "insubstantial." He feels Trollope always "just eludes being serious" and almost always "escapes being really humorous." He dismisses Alice Vavasor's problems as trivial, and notes that the novel should be about Glencora. Burgo and George are both dismissed abruptly from the novel instead of being properly developed.

65. —. *Nation*, 2 (4 January, 1866), 21.

Review of *The Belton Estate*. James opens by noting that there is nothing new in this plot but that this novel is "more readable than many of its predecessors." He observes with pleasure that there are no subplots, then rather disparagingly outlines the main story. He feels that all of Trollope's work has a flatness, and all his readers know this; it is useless to complain of it. Will Belton is described as the best character, though all of them suffer from the lack of a mind. "Our great objection to 'The Belton Estate' is that, as we read it, we seemed to be reading a book written for children." He explains this opinion by noting that it is stupid rather than dull, as the novel is "without a single idea."

66. Unsigned. "An Amateur Theologian," *Saturday Review*, 21 (3 February, 1866), 131-133.

This writer chides Trollope for an article the latter wrote in the *Fortnightly Review* (Cf. T21) on the sabbatarian controversy. He remarks that Trollope is a very good novelist, and not a theologian at all. He does not criticize the ideas in Trollope's article, but he terms them commonplace and not worth the space they were given. He notes that Trollope also made several obvious errors, and in fact wrote a very ignorant article about a view that was not worth attacking.

67. Unsigned. "Reviews," *Saturday Review*, 21 (3 February, 1866), 140-142.

Review of *The Belton Estate*. This reviewer criticizes Trollope for repeating the same old plot he has used before — a lady between two suitors. He notes that a painter could never get away with repeating a painting he had already done, and authors should not escape either. While Trollope is right to stay with the same general topic (the feelings of young and middle-aged ladies) because he is so good at it, he is wrong to continue to have the same conflict, the reviewer feels. He claims that the description of Alice Vavasor could be used verbatim in the presentation of Clara. The reviewer insists that Trollope should write less often, to maintain a freshness and vivacity in his novels. He also faults Trollope for the lack of really heroic characters — in *The Belton Estate*, even those who win what they want in the end are really petty and crude.

68. [Wilberforce]. "Reviews," *Athenaeum* no. 1997 (3 February, 1866), 166.

Review of *The Belton Estate*. Wilberforce points out that once again Trollope's plot turns on two men, different in character, who are in pursuit of the same woman. The woman seems not quite credible in that her "admiration for frankness" wins out over "natural, womanly instinct" in her choice of a husband. Wilberforce feels that Will Belton is too full of swagger and "rude nature" to be a suitable hero. There are, nonetheless, some outstanding scenes.

69. [Alford, Henry]. "Mr. Anthony Trollope and the English Clergy," *Contemporary Review*, 2 (June, 1866), 240-262.

Review of a series of articles by Trollope which appeared in the *Pall Mall Gazette* and were later published as *Clergymen of the Church of England*. The reviewer refers to "this book of Mr. Trollope's" as seriously uninformed, indeed, "entirely ignorant," obviously intended to attract a wide audience rather than to represent a true case. One must judge very harshly the motives of a writer who does not check his facts. The reviewer attacks several allegations made by Trollope in the series, and attacks Trollope himself for making such statements. He mentions several clerical practices which he himself deplores (the purchasing and use of prepared sermons, for example) but defends the clergy as, on the whole, a highly moral group. He does find Trollope's final chapter, on the Colenso affair, to be well done.

70. Unsigned. "Mr. Anthony Trollope and Curates' Stipends," *Pall Mall Gazette*, 4 (20 June, 1866), 217.

The writer takes note of the series of articles, "The Clergymen of the Church of England," which Trollope had authored earlier in the year for this journal, and some letters criticizing it as inaccurate which readers had submitted. This writer has researched the matter and finds that the evidence shows that in fact curates are as badly paid as Trollope had asserted. The writer regrets that this is the case, but announces that he takes pride in the *Pall Mall Gazette* having been proven correct and the angry letter-writers, and a columnist in the *Guardian* having been refuted.

71. Unsigned. "*The Belton Estate,* By Anthony Trollope," *Contemporary Review,* 3 (October, 1866), 300-302.

This reviewer declares that Trollope is "the most readable of novelists, with the exception of Mr. Charles Reade, who may take even rank with him." He praises Trollope's characterizations of women and his capacity for not violating decorum or good taste in his fiction: writers like this do a public service by helping the "ordinary people" not to "fall back" into bad taste or inferior values. This novel, he feels, while not notably weaker than Trollope's others, has a "paleness" when compared to his early fiction. The reviewer discusses scenes in the novel as though certain that the reader is familiar with them. He concludes, "we like Mr. Trollope, and *The Belton Estate* is a good, interesting story, brightly told, and full of touches of true English feeling."

72. [Chorley, Henry F.] "Reviews," *Athenaeum* no. 2053 (2 March, 1867), 288.

Review of *Nina Balatka.* Chorley offers a synopsis of the plot, noting that it "is told so clearly and tersely, and with so much real feeling, as to retain the reader to the last." He notes that the "study of character" is here more important than the plot itself.

73. [Wise, J. R.] "Contemporary Literature: Belles Lettres," *Westminster Review,* 87, o.s. (April, 1867), 273.

Review of *Nina Balatka.* The review finds this novel to be outstanding "for knowledge of human nature and especially for power in drawing certain types of men." The book is particularly recommended for country libraries, "where really healthy novels are so much wanted."

74. Unsigned. "Reviews," *Saturday Review,* 23 (18 May, 1867), 638-639.

Review of *The Claverings*. The review opens with a discussion of the reasons for Trollope's continued popularity and interest despite the lack of real movement or excitement in his fiction. It is suggested that the truthfulness of pictures and the fairness of Trollope's conclusions are responsible. Trollope's conclusions, the reviewer notes, are comforting to us: we are sure Julia will get what she deserves, but will not be totally destroyed. He applauds Trollope for not resorting to 'deus ex machina' devices to get his novels ended satisfactorily. Everyone in this novel does suffer, but those who do the right thing eventually triumph. He mentions that some of the minor characters — Sir Hugh, Archie, and Boodle — are perfectly drawn. He concludes that Trollope always writes honest and artistic works.

75. Knight, J. "Critical Notices," *Fortnightly Review*, 7 (June, 1867), 770-772.

Review of *The Claverings*. Here, the reviewer says, Anthony Trollope's gift for realism "seems to have reached its limits. Confining himself to actual life in England . . . Mr. Trollope scorns and rejects all extraneous aid whatever." He compares Trollope's effects to those of Balzac; both use many tiny details to create a "perfect" picture. While Balzac deals with the heart and brain, however, Trollope works with "the nerves just under the skin." The reviewer then summarizes the plot of *The Claverings* and praises the characterization.

76. [Jewsbury, Geraldine]. "Reviews," *Athenaeum*, no. 2068 (15 June, 1867), 783.

Review of *The Claverings*. Jewsbury declares that this novel is "not so entertaining" as others by Trollope, but it is admirable for its "artistic workmanship." She praises Trollope for the "sketches of character and slight episodes which are masterpieces . . . true to life and to human nature." She defends Trollope's lightness, noting that if the story had been one of "deeper studies in human nature," it "might not have been so pleasant to read."

77. [Wise, J. R.] "Contemporary Literature: Belles Lettres," *Westminster Review*, 88 (July, 1867), 145.

Review of *The Last Chronicle of Barset*. Wise has faint praise for Trollope here: "his descriptions, though wanting in all high artistic power, seldom violate good taste. His philosophy, though a series of commonplaces, never particularly offends . . . ." He notes that many "old, familiar" characters reappear in this novel, and recommends it to those who enjoy reading Trollope.

78. Unsigned. "Anthony Trollope on Female Character," *Pall Mall Gazette*, 6 (27 July, 1867), 373.

The author of this article begins by attributing a remark to Trollope, to the effect that for a man to win a man's respect, he must abuse himself verbally to the other man; but to win a woman's respect, he should abuse or belittle her. This writer anticipates that women readers will be outrgaed at such an idea, and may lose much of their fondness for Trollope's work if they sense that this is in fact his attitude. The writer proceeds to speculate on the ramifications of Trollope's alleged assertion, noting that women could certainly abuse men in modern English society, but probably could not, and do not seem to, abuse other women.

79. [Jewsburgy, Geraldine]. "Reviews," *Athenaeum*, no. 2075 (3 August, 1867), 141.

Review of *The Last Chronicle of Barset*. This novel Jewsbury regards as "carefully written," inhabited by characters who "have remarkable substance and vitality." She notes that all of the Barchester novels are "singularly real in their interest, and veraciously like Nature." She remarks on the widespread public interest in these characters (to the point that some feel a real friendship for them). She finds the Conway Dalrymple episode, however, "quite disagreeable," and incongruous with the rest of the story.

80. [Oliphant, Margaret]. "Novels," *Blackwood's Edinburgh Magazine,* 52 (September, 1867), 275-278.

    Oliphant begins with an extended criticism of recent novels: too many heroines appear whose thoughts and actions are improper and sensational. Of *The Claverings,* she says that although the plot is far from new, Trollope's style is so pleasant that the reader does not mind. She finds that Trollope does sometimes misrepresent modern women, who "are neither so passive nor so grateful as they are made out to be." She good-naturedly twits Trollope for having Mrs. Proudie die, and for ending the Barchester series. She praises the Reverend Crawley as a "superb" characterization, and remarks that Trollope has beautified the world with his characters.

81. Unsigned. "Lotta Schmidt," *Saturday Review,* 24 (21 September, 1867), 381-382.

    Review of *Lotta Schmidt and Other Stories.* Although one would not expect it, this reviewer notes, "Mr Trollope is as successful in his short stories as in his longer novels." He describes this collection as "pleasant fancies of the thinnest material worked up with the smallest expenditure of labour possible – not strong meat, by any means, but clean and wholesome milk." He summarizes the plots of several of the stories, and comments that Trollope is to be commended for the "facile painting" here, if not the high art.

82. Unsigned. "Reviews," *Pall Mall Gazette,* 8 (19 August, 1868), 565.

    Review of *Linda Tressel.* The writer's citation attributes the authorship of the book, as the publisher does, to "the author of *Nina Balatka*," but indicates that "the author betrays himself unmistakably in every page," and the reviewer expresses wonder that the novel's author does not openly admit his authorship. Unlike most contemporary novels, which this reviewer alleges "enfeeble the mind," *Linda Tressel* he finds "as healthful as it is pleasant." He admires the fact that the love plot is incidental, not central, to the story, and praises the characterization and the capacity of the story to captivate the interest of the reader. He concludes that this novel is certainly worthy of the novelist's reputation.

83. [Percy, G.] "Mr. Trollope's Novels," *National Review*, 7 (October, 1868), 416-435.

Percy begins by noting that novels have replaced romances as the type of fiction in popular demand. Fiction is now "laid among quiet homes . . . . They are dramatic rather than narrative," and "they are tales of character," not of incident or manners. He continues that novels are interesting, if not exciting, and they have a moral point. He puts Trollope among the best living novelists. He praises *The Warden* and *Barchester Towers*, and recounts their plots in some detail. He finds fault with *The Three Clerks* for being too digressive, and with *Dr. Thorne* for inadequate character development. He concludes that Trollope has the power to be a truly great novelist, largely because of his attention to minute detail.

84. Stack, J. H. "Mr. Anthony Trollope's Novels," *Fortnightly Review*, 5, n.s. (1 February, 1869), 188-198.

Stack begins with a discussion of the question of photographic realism as art. He asserts that Trollope often does better than "mere" realism in his fiction, and cites *The Last Chronicle of Barset* as an example. He gives a plot summary and comments on the tragic quality of the situation of Mr. Crawley. His only annoyance is at Lily Dale being "trotted out again" in this story, and he wishes the whole Eames-Dale-Crosbie situation were omitted. *The Warden*, he feels, is Trollope's second best novel; there are no irrelevant people or incidents. While much of Trollope's work may not survive its age, that will be because his work is so solidly of one time and place. The kind of clergy he draws so well are even at the time of this review disappearing from the scene. He could have written "more of a story" if he had had Glencora run away with Burgo Fitzgerald; as readers, this reviewer thinks, we would like our souls to "be purged by terror, and pity, and stronger thoughts than amusement at unmarried jilts, married flirts, and young mothers."

85. Unsigned. "He Knew He Was Right," *Saturday Review*, 27 (June, 1869), 751-753.

Over his career, this reviewer says, Trollope has deserved an award for human industry in a good cause. His novels are not regarded as spiced meat, but are healthy and very appetizing nonetheless. This novel, the reviewer states, is quite readable, though it would be enlivened by one heroic, or even mildly heroic, character. Too many of Trollope's romances are staged like a painting of an ass between two bales of hay. Men, he complains, are almost always feeble-minded as lovers in Trollope's works. He feels that there are too many characters in this novel, and recounts the plot, concluding that, even with its faults, it has much for Trollope fans to enjoy.

86. [Wise, J. R.] "Contemporary Literature: Belles Lettres," *Westminster Review*, 92 (July, 1869), 144-145.

Review of *He Knew He Was Right*. This reviewer notes that novels in general are rather repetitious and cites Trollope's works as an illustration; he feels that Trollope's modest talents have been exhausted, and that he never did have much of "high spirits, humour, nor satire," and has been popular because of his "photographic power." In this novel, he says, Trollope has weak and unreal characters, and a feeble, sometimes "repulsive" plot; but it is nonetheless a "readable tale."

87. Unsigned. "Literary Notes," *Appleton's Journal of Literature, Science, and Art,* I (August 7, 1869), 603.

This entry is a notation and summary of the review of *He Knew He Was Right,* which appears in the recent issue of *The Spectator.*

88. [Broome, F. N.] "He Knew He Was Right," London *Times,* 26 August, 1869, p. 4.

The reviewer opens by noting the great number and success of Trollope's works, and their similarity. *He Knew He Was Right* is described as "shapeless as a boned fowl, entirely without any skeleton of plot." Lack of plot is viewed by this reviewer as a virtue, as it distinguishes this sort of novel from sensational fiction. *Framley Parsonage* is cited as another plotless and entertaining novel. The "commonplace" elements are a positive feature, he feels, although in this novel he would like to see a strong character; there are not many people here whom he would wish to know. The Barchester series are perfect novels, he feels; although the arguments are sometimes tedious, and the dialogue is generally not so accurate as in Trollope's earlier works. Overall, he feels that Trollope's work is so good that it invites hypercriticism.

89. [Hoey, J. C. (and prob. F. Hoey)]. "Mr. Trollope's Last Irish Novel," *Dublin Review,* 65, o.s. (October, 1869), 361-377.

Review of *Phineas Finn.* This review begins with an extended discussion of and praise for Trollope's earlier Irish novels, and his mastery of characterization and truth of setting. The review notes that the Irish clergy are generally more admirable people than the English clergy in Trollope's other novels. *Phineas Finn* is praised for its characterization and dialogue.

90. Unsigned. "British Sports and Pastimes," *Saturday Review*, 28 (13 November, 1869), 652-654.

Review of *British Sports and Pastimes*, edited by Trollope. The essay on hunting, which Trollope wrote for this collection, "is decidedly the best of the essays," according to the reviewer. He praises it as having many practical hints, a frank discussion of the necessary expenses, a defense of hunting as relatively safe, and as perfectly appropriate for clergymen.

91. Taylor, Helen. "A Few Words on Mr. Trollope's Defence of Fox-hunting," *Fortnightly Review*, 13, o.s. (January, 1870), 63-68.

Taylor responds here to an article by Trollope in *Fortnightly Review*. She quotes some of his arguments in favor of the sport of fox-hunting and offers a rebuttal.

92. [Oliphant, Margaret]. "New Books," *Blackwood's Edinburgh Magazine*, 112 (May, 1870), 647-648.

Review of *The Vicar of Bulhampton*. Oliphant praises Trollope's "vivaciousness and inexhaustible imagination," especially in the Barchester series. She finds this new novel "indecorous" and therefore does not recommend it. Mary Lowther's behavior in breaking two engagements is unjustifiably defended, she feels, by Tollope: "The less we hear about such people, the better off we are." She does not, however, object to the substantial part played in the novel by the prostitute, Carrie Brattle. She asks Trollope to write again about such people as inhabit the Barchester novels.

93. Towle, G. M. "Anthony Trollope," *Appleton's Journal of Popular Literature, Science, and Art*, 3 (May 14, 1870), 551-553.

Towle opens his article with a mention of Mrs. Trollope's book on America and its shortcomings; he notes that she has two writer-sons, Thomas, the novelist and historian, and Anthony, the "most talented member of a talented family." Towle considers that Anthony is now "the most popular of living novelists," and offers a list of his publications, noting also that his editorship of *St. Paul's* magazine made it a "rival of *Macmillan's* and *The Cornhill*." He notes that Trollope is "a true artist of the commonplace," and is true to the experience of young people, avoiding always the sensational. Towle feels that Trollope lacks the "brilliancy" of Bulwer, the vividness of Reade, the humor of Dickens, and the satire of Thackeray, but has considerable talent and has made a real contribution to literature in his characterization of clergymen.

94. Unsigned. "The Vicar of Bulhampton," *Saturday Review*, 29 (14 May, 1870), 646-647.

This reviewer opens by remarking on the "fecundity" of several contemporary authors, Trollope among them. This story is criticized as having no plot and no connection between the two groups of people in it. There are no pleasant people in either group, the reviewer complains. Although Captain Marrable's father did certainly wrong him, "we don't like to hear a son call his father a swindler and a liar to his face," nor should such a son win the heroine of the story. The reviewer offers a synopsis, insisting again that the novel is plotless though he finds a few good scenes and some "caustic humour." He concludes, nonetheless, that "Mr. Trollope's third-rate is more readable than most novelists' best."

95. Unsigned. "The Parson of Mr. Trollope's Novels," *Every Saturday* (2nd series) I (May 28, 1870), 347-349.

This reviewer commends the variety and richness of Trollope's presentation of clergy: "his surest card, his theme on which there is always something new to say that is worth saying." This writer comments on the clerics in the works of Dickens, Kingsley, Bulwer, and Thackeray, noting that they all pale before those of Trollope. Several of Trollope's clergy are then briefly described, with laudatory comments about their realistic portrayal.

96. Unsigned. "Mr. Trollope's Last Novel," London *Times*, 3 June, 1870, p. 4.

Review of *The Vicar of Bulhampton*. The *Times* reviewer presents a reather detailed plot summary, and judges Mary Lowther to be "the most provoking" heroine ever, and her story to be rather tedious.

97. [Wise, J. R.] "Contemporary Literature," *Westminster Review*, 94 (July, 1870), 102.

Review of *The Commentaries of Caesar*. In this very brief mention of the work, Trollope is said to "dilate on the merits and shortcomings of the man who, in his judgment, has done the most to move the world."

98. Unsigned. "Anthony Trollope's *Ancient Classics for English Readers: The Commentaries of Caesar*," *Pall Mall Gazette*, 12 (18 July, 1870), 972.

This writer commends the book as having a "racy" style characteristic of Trollope; he also praises Trollope's "purpose of making this wonderful work" of Caesar's familiar to readers unable to deal with the Latin original. The reviewer thinks perhaps Trollope over-values Caesar's contributions to history, and judges that a real understanding of the *Commentaries* can be achieved only by reading the original text. However, he feels, readers will "gain some food for thought and many novel suggestions from the writer's vigorous and pictureque handling of the history."

He particularly commends Trollope's frequent comparison of events and problems of Caesar's time to current English situations, although Trollope's familiar style of writing may be somewhat misleading to readers, as the original text is quite formal.

99. Unsigned. "An Editor's Tales," *Saturday Review,* 30 (13 August, 1870), 211-212.

This article opens with a remark on the quantity of Trollope's literary works and their usually respectable level of quality. The reviewer notes that Trollope does often fail to achieve an "artistic unity of effect," because his stories wander. He then recounts the tales in this collection, commenting that they are "a trifle dull," with the exception of "The Spotted Dog," a truly good story.

100. Unsigned. "Caesar's Commentaries," London *Times*, 13 August, 1870, p. 12.

This reviewer admires the motivation of the series of which this volume is a part and of Trollope in serving those who do not read Latin. The only fault he finds is that the book is perhaps too deliberately un-scholarly. The tone seems to him sometimes condescending; but on the whole he finds it a "handy little book."

101. Unsigned. "A Vacant Throne," *Literary World,* 1 (September, 1870), 56.

This article speculates on the possible successors to Dickens as the universally accepted "king" of English fiction. Trollope and Wilkie Collins are admittedly the most prominent of current novelists, but the writer feels neither has adequate genius to fill Dickens' place. George Eliot, he concludes, is the only logical choice as the country's most distinguished writer of fiction.

102. [Wise, J. R.] "Contemporary Literature," *Westminster Review*, 94 (October, 1870), 248.

Review of *An Editor's Tales*. The writer remarks on Trollope's industry and disparages generally his non-fiction writing. This collection, he says, is especially charming. He offers synopses of the tales in the volumes, and notes that a new edition of *He Knew He Was Right* is now available.

103. Unsigned. "Sir Harry Hotspur of Humblethwaite," London *Times*, 16 November, 1870, p. 4.

This review begins with an extended plot recapitulation. The reviewer praises the novel as vigorous, but notes that it might not be suitable for young people to read. However, overly fond mothers would be well-advised, he thinks, to take the lesson offered by the story.

104. Unsigned. "Sir Harry Hotspur of Humblethwaite," *Saturday Review*, 30 (10 December, 1870), 753-755.

This reviewer complains that neither the author nor the reader seems to care for the hero or the heroine in this novel, as "every body is in the wrong." The novel, he asserts, is an anti-aristocratic "satire, veiling a serious if not a fierce meaning." He describes the story, noting all the vices of the characters. This novel, he notes, does show signs of careful composition, unlike some of Trollope's other works.

105. Unsigned. "Contemporary Literature: Belles Lettres," *Westminster Review*, 95 (Janury, 1871), 130.

Review of *An Editor's Tales*. This reviewer makes a brief mention of the tales, and about Trollope's remarkable ability to create sympathy for characters who are weak or foolish. The only fault he finds here is wordiness.

106. Unsigned. Untitled. *Literary World*, 1 (March, 1871), 149-150.

Review of *Sir Harry Hotspur of Humblethwaite*. This writer finds it amazing that Trollope can tell a story in such a short space as he does with this one. Although there are no old, familiar characters in this novel, the reviewer finds "the same wearisome minuteness of detail, the same prolix analyses of mental operations, the same sameness of characteristics, which is the common property of all his girls." After presenting a summary of the plot, the writer expresses some surprise at Trollope's popularity in the light of the similarity of all his stories to each other, and the fact that Trollope "plays with ideas as a cat with a mouse."

107. Wise, J. R. "Contemporary Literature," *Westminster Review*, 95 (April, 1871), 273.

Review of *The Struggles of Brown, Jones, and Robinson, By One of the Firm*. The reviewer gives this novel very short shrift, declares it "unmitigated rubbish." The chief faults he finds are coarseness and unsuccessful satire.

108. [Bristead, C. A.] Untitled Review. *North American Review*, 112 (April, 1871), 433-441.

Review of *Ralph the Heir*. Bristead notes that the novel is appearing serially, and the conclusion has not yet been published. But thus far, he feels, this novel refutes the rumor that Trollope has "written himself out," as it is as good as novels by Thackeray or Dickens. Bristead thinks Trollope's excellence lies in the depiction of "the general walk and conversation of the upper and upper-middle classes," and especially in his accounts of the ways in which they quarrel. A further virtue, the reviewer finds, is that the dull or stupid characters are yet believable. He goes on to observe that America has not produced so good a novelist, and speculates that this may be so because the social classes in America are more distinct from each other and have less contact with each other than is the case in England. Americans, he feels, jealously cling to their own sets and cliques, and thus their interests and appreciations are narrower than those of the English. American writers excel, he feels, at adventure stories and psychological romances, but are not convincing realists.

109. [Collyer]. "Reviews," *Athenaeum,* no. 2268 (15 April, 1871), 456.

Review of *Ralph the Heir.* Collyer points out that this novel is analogous to "portraits in the costume of this period," such as might be exhibited at a museum. He praises Trollope's ability to show the foibles and "little self-deceptions" of society. *Ralph the Heir* has some good moments, he grants, but the reviewer finally "cannot admire it."

110. Unsigned. "Ralph the Heir," London *Times,* 17 April, 1871, p. 6.

An extended summary of the novel opens this review, with the wry comment: "Ralph the Heir is the least interesting person in the story; at last we are rather glad of a chapter in which he does not appear." The election and courtship sequences are highly praised as truthful and humourous. The reviewer declares that this novel shows no signs that Trollope's writing power are declining.

111. Unsigned. "Ralph the Heir," *Saturday Review,* 31 (29 April, 1871), 537-538.

The review opens with a recommendation of this novel as pleasant, and as superior to some of Trollope's past works. The reviewer notes that this work is marked by a "genial humour" and by new characters. Neefit the tailor is a memorable character because he is seen to move and act; the Newtons are less memorable. He recounts the plot, enumerates the principal characters, and concludes that this is "a marvel of freshness."

112. Unsigned. "Novels of the Week," *Athenaeum*, no. 2326 (25 May, 1872), 651-653.

Review of *The Golden Lion of Granpere*. This review is largely a commentary on the principal characters in the novel and their truth to human nature. The reviewer feels that Marie is an especially admirable heroine. He praises the sense of humor apparent in the novel, and terms it "an excellent tale." English readers will, he thinks, find the setting very appealing.

113. Unsigned. "Anthony Trollope," *Once A Week*, 9 (June, 1872), 498-500.

This article opens with some remarks about Frances Trollope and her "interesting and clever" books and then proceeds to a consideration of her son's work. Trollope's mastery at the portrayal of clergy is noted, and attributed in part to the fact that Anthony's grandfather was a parson. The reviewer lauds Trollope's treatment of dialogue as "exactly like life." After listing all of Trollope's publications to date, he judges that they are below the "high mark of the great writers" but are all interesting and display "good, sound art in their manipulation." Trollope is judged comparable to Mrs. Wood and Miss Braddon in writing realistically and amusingly.

114. Unsigned. "The Golden Lion of Granpere," *Saturday Review*, 33 (29 June, 1872), 833-835.

This reviewer notes that Trollope writes even when on vacation, as he seems to have taken advantage of a holiday in Alsace to produce this novel. The reviewer finds the work flawed, however, by the author's inadequate knowledge of the people and customs of the region he chose as a setting. The heroine here seems much more like an English Protestant than an Alsatian Catholic, he feels. Trollope is very good, he notes, at describing what he sees, but he did not adequately understand or describe the character of family life, personal relationships, and religious feeling here. The reviewer discusses some of the characters central to the plot, and reiterates the weaknesses caused, he feels, by Trollope's minimal experience of Alsace.

115. Reade, Charles. "Ralph the Heir." *Pall Mall Gazette*, 16 (July, 1872), 357.

In a letter to the editor, Mr. Reade comments about a recently produced play, "Shilly Shally," written by himself but bearing Trollope's name as author; he had done this with the more prominent author's permission. He states that he now understands that Trollope objects to this use of his name, so Reade will remove it. He wishes, however, to attribute the invention of "those excellent characters and natural dialogues whose dramatic value his (i.e., Trollope's) modesty has so undervalued" to their true source, Anthony Trollope.

116. Unsigned. "Old Maids," *Blackwood's Edinburgh Magazine*, 112 (July, 1872), 92-108.

This article, on spinsterhood and attitudes toward it, has a brief discussion of Trollope's *Dr. Thorne*. Most novelists, the writer claims, are in favor of women marrying beneath themselves socially, especially if the alternative is not to marry at all; however, *Dr. Thorne* is cited as being opposed to this prevalent notion. The writer points out that Amelia de Courcey, after advising Miss Gresham not to marry the attorney Gazebee, later marries him herself, and Amelia is not an admirable figure in the novel.

117. Unsigned. Untitled, *Literary World*, 3 (August, 1872), 42-43.

Review of *The Golden Lion of Granpere*. "This is not the best of the author's stories . . ." begins this reviewer, noting that although the ostensible setting is Lorraine, it could as easily be called "Devonshire or New Jersey," as it is not distinctively presented. The reviewer outlines the novel's plot, remarking that the heroine alone of the characters is outstanding, and that there is too much preaching in the story. He concludes that this is a pleasant but not brilliant novel, and suggests it as adequate entertainment for a "hot August afternoon."

118. [Hoey, Frances C. ?] "The Novels of Mr. Anthony Trollope," *Dublin Review*, 71, o.s. (October, 1872), 393-430.

Hoey deals with virtually all the earlier works, citing those through *Can You Forgive Her?* She judges Trollope to be the master of the novel, as distinguished from the romance by its realistic portraiture. Even George Eliot, she feels, who is more intellectual, is not truer in detail than is Trollope. Hoey classes Trollope as superior to Wilkie Collins and Herman Melville, and in certain ways even to Thackeray and Dickens. She has distinct praise for *The MacDermotts of Ballycloran, The Kellys and The O'Kellys,* and *Castle Richmond* for their faithfulness to the details of Irish character and setting. She criticizes the treatment of religion and clergy in the other novels: debates upon theological points are incomplete and unsatisfactory; even Mr. Harding is not a truly religious man, and Mr. Arabin's thoughts on the Oxford Movement are not probable nor admirable. Trollope's girls, she finds, are all too similar; his mature women are more skillfully drawn. Although she thinks him prejudiced against the aristocracy, she praises his strong sense of humor.

119. Unsigned. "Reviews," *Westminster Review*, 98 (October, 1872), 268.

This item is not really a review, but rather a listing of new editions; among those cited are *The Small House at Allington, Framley Parsonage,* and *The Claverings.*

120. Unsigned. "The Eustace Diamonds," London *Times*, 30 October, 1872, p. 4.

The reviewer praises this novel as equal to any of Trollope's previous works, but finds three faults with it: this Lucy is too similar to the Lucy of *Framley Parsonage*; the story is too drawn-out; and Lucinda Roanoke's broken-off marriage should have been deleted. The reviewer finds it otherwise an "excellent novel," and gives an account of the principal characters and plot.

121. Unsigned. Untitled. *Literary World*, 3 (November, 1872), 86.

Review of *The Eustace Diamonds*. This writer approves of the departure from the conventional Barchester romance which he perceives here. After a short plot outline, the reviewer complains that there is no character in the novel worthy of admiration except Lucy Morris. He disapproves of the Pallisers' presence as pointless, and of the novel as too lengthy. For all this, though, the reviewer admits finding the novel interesting, though not equal to one of Wilkie Collins' detective stories.

122. Unsigned. "The Eustace Diamonds," *Saturday Review*, 34 (16 November, 1872), 637-638.

"Mr. Trollope is himself again," this reviewer notes with relief. Here, he thinks Trollope has tried to make a rival of Becky Sharp in Lizzie. Although the story seems to betray a low estimation of humanity, honesty does prove to be the best policy. Lizzie is brilliantly drawn, the reviewer notes, and he describes her character in some length. He finds the hero a very questionable personage, however, as he is a "contemptible figure." No true hero would have philandered with Lizzie himself while being engaged to Lucie Morris. The great amount of description, in place of direct action, is a disappointment to this reviewer, as is the repetitiousness. He further finds that the Lucinda Roanoke affair has no excuse for being in a novel at all. All in all, however, the novel is both amusing and instructive.

123. Unsigned. "Mr. Trollope's Australia and New Zealand," London *Times*, 12 April, 1873, p. 7.

The *Times* reviewer cites this as the best account yet published of these two countries, even though it is flawed by repetitiousness: "every opinion is stated at least twice, and some even one hundred times." Despite this failing, however, the book is declared full of important information for British readers about a part of the world they should know about. The reviewer gives a synopsis of the two-volume work and praises Trollope's abilities as a raconteur and an adventurer.

124. Unsigned. "Trollope's Australia and New Zealand," *Saturday Review*, 35 (26 April, 1873), 554-555.

The reviewer notes that this work is already in its second edition, but he had insisted on reading the lengthy work through before writing a review. Trollope has, he thinks, compiled a blue-book here, and is playing at being a political analyst and economist. The reviewer finds that Trollope has much that is worthwhile to say, though "he is frequently commonplace." The reviewer thinks that here Trollope has underestimated his readers, and he over-explains and talks down to them; thus this reviewer finds the book tiresome to read. Another weakness found here is the result of Trollope's writing as he went along on his trip, rather than waiting to consolidate his ideas. The reviewer dislikes the great part that statistics and authorial theories have in the work and wishes there were more physical description of the lands. He concludes that Trollope had a good intention, but produced "an amorphous mass of writing."

125. Unsigned. "Mr. Trollope on Novels," *Saturday Review*, 36 (22 November, 1873), 656-657.

This article is written in response to a second-hand report of a talk given by Trollope to "some youthful students" on the subject of the morality of novels. Trollope considers novels, the writer has heard, to be the sermons of the modern day. The reviewer feels that this fact may account for the great dullness of many contemporary novels, though Trollope's works are not among the dull ones. The reviewer further feels that the principle of poetic justice is edifying to a point, but is often unrealistic; not all villains are punished as they deserve, and authors should not pretend otherwise. The reviewer speculates that what Trollope means is that, for example, we can "learn to love manliness" from Walter Scott, and "learn to hate meanness" from Thackeray. The reviewer objects strongly to the creation of novels for propagandistic or political ends. Trollope's novels, he comments, do give the idea that life is on the whole manageable and the world is filled with many pleasant and honest people and some who are less than this. Many novelists are not so convincing. Too many novels are published, and many of them are too inferior to exercise the intellect; this reviewer decries the current trend of indiscriminate novel-publishing and novel-reading. He wishes that Trollope had addressed the issues of the criteria for judging fiction, and the place of novel-reading in an intelligent person's life instead of this general topic.

126. Unsigned. "Mr. Trollope on Novels," *Every Saturday,* 4th series, 1 (January, 1874), 22-24.

This article is a reprint of the preceding article (entry 125).

127. Unsigned. "Phineas Redux," *Saturday Review,* 37 (7 February, 1874), 186-187.

The reviewer begins by wondering whether this is properly called a novel, as it has no plot, and all the characters are past 30 years old. He notes that it is, in fact, more amusing than most novels are, and is solid evidence that Trollope is again himself. Trollope's perfect familiarity with these characters allows a thoroughness of conception which is the secret of their success with the readers. The reviewer discusses the character of Phineas, noting that his bravery is not compromised by the breakdown he suffers after the trial: in fact, that breakdown makes him more believable. The reviewer concludes that there is much in the novel that is very well done, including its satire of the Conservative party.

128. [Dicey, A. V.] "Anthony Trollope," *The Nation*, 18 (March 12, 1874), 174-175.

General review of Trollope's works. Dicey comments on the number and speed of Trollope's productions, and adds, "But he never produces work made simply to sell." He notes that Trollope writes for those readers whose taste is "too good to be satisfied with Miss Braddon, and not good enough to enjoy George Eliot." He criticizes Trollope as "absolutely unable to devise a plot," and cites as examples of this failing the treatment of Phineas Finn in *Phineas Redux*. Dicey considers Trollope less inventive than Dickens and lacking in the ability to create "vivid amusement;" however, he does not consider these "fatal defects." Trollope's worst failing is his inability to create original characters such as Becky Sharp or Dorothea Brooke. Thackeray and Balzac had an "intellectual truthfulness" which Dicey does not find in Trollope, as he has not successfully described the workings of human feelings. Lady Laura should be a profoundly tragic woman, but is only superficially dealt with by her author. Trollope's success, the reviewer feels, depends on two characteristics: "unrivalled power of depicting manners" and the author's common-sensible observations. These qualities contribute to an easy intelligibility, and easy optimism about the present state of English society.

129. Unsigned. Untitled. *Literary World*, 4 (April, 1874), 172.

Review of *Phineas Redux*. The writer considers this novel's title absurd because it assumes that everyone can read and understand Latin. The story, however, he finds a very interesting political tale, despite its prolixity. There are "graphic pictures of parliamentary life, and striking portraits of Messrs. Gladstone and Disraeli (Gresham and Daubeny)," which make it well worth reading.

130. Unsigned. "Lady Anna," *Saturday Review*, 37 (9 May, 1874), 598-599.

The reviewer thinks that Trollope must have known this would be an unpopular theme even as he wrote the novel. He discusses the characters of both Anna and the tailor, and notes that George Eliot's *Felix Holt* could succeed because the hero is not so coarse as is Trollope's tailor. The purpose of fiction, he contends, is to teach by pleasing; this novel will fail even to please. He thinks the rumor that Trollope wrote this story on a bet may explain the attempt. He suggests how the characters might have been conceived so as to make this story successful, and points out a number of unlikely incidents and faults of character in this novel.

131. Unsigned. Untitled, *Literary World*, 5 (October, 1874), 70.

Review of *New Zealand*. This reviewer finds that Trollope is not prolix here, and has produced a very interesting work indeed. Trollope proves himself to be "a discriminating observer." The reviewer notes that this volume is part of a larger work, *Australia and New Zealand*, which has not been reprinted in the United States. Trollope's synopsis of the history of New Zealand is praised, and the contents of the volume are outlined. The reviewer notes one "stupendous blunder" on Trollope's part in a remark on the rules governing U. S. statehood, but concludes that it is a valuable work.

132. Unsigned, *Athenaeum*, no. 2454 (November, 1874), 606.

Review of *Harry Heathcote of Gangoil.* This brief review notes with approval Trollope's "minuteness of observation." The story is deprecated as "too slight to add to the author's reputation," although the writer feels "it will not diminish" Trollope's reputation either. The character of the hero and his difficulties are described to support the reviewer's judgment.

133. Unsigned. "Harry Heathcote of Gangoil," *Saturday Review,* 38 (7 November, 1874), 609-610.

The reviewer notes in opening that here is the pith of Trollope's book about Australia, in a more entertaining form. He summarizes the plot and suggests that the villains are too mild-mannered, the fights too tame, to be really convincing. Kingsley, he feels, is better at scenic description than Trollope is in this novel. He notes with chagrin that not even one kangaroo appears in the story. The hero is deserving of praise, however, as he has the advantages of muscular Christians without being offensively virtuous. The heroines of Trollope all need a little more intellect, he feels, though for the minimal place they have here they are adequate. He offers a summary of the plot, stopping short of revealing the outcome lest he spoil the story for potential readers.

134. Unsigned. "Contemporary Literature: Belles Lettres," *Westminster Review,* American edition, 103 (April, 1875), 268.

Review of *Harry Heathcote of Gangoil.* This reviewer notes that there is "nothing whatever" in this novel except another example of Trollope's versatility, "as if that were needed." He rates Trollope as inferior to Charles Kingsley, but feels certain that this will be a popular adventure story with young boys.

135. [Collyer]. "Novels of the Week," *Athenaeum,* no. 2487 (25 June, 1875), 85.

Review of *The Way We Live Now.* Collyer finds many faults

with this novel, declaring it "not one of his best, and apparently he has bestowed little pains upon it." Trollope's "ignorance of the limits of his capacities" is proved, the reviewer asserts, by his choice of a swindler as the "hero of the tale." The book's structure is criticized as weak and unbalanced, although the characterization of the Longstaffes is noted as "excellent."

136. Unsigned. "The Way We Live Now," *Saturday Review*, 40 (17 July, 1875), 88-89.

The reviewer opens by objecting to the "we" in the title, insisting that he, at least, is not a part of the group mentioned. He describes Melmotte as the hero, and a swindler "who rises almost into respectability." He notes that it is impossible not to sympathize in a degree with someone who struggles so hard and so unceasingly, though in an evil direction. The novel should have a foil character to oppose Melmotte morally, he feels; the satire intended loses some of its effect by reason of this lack. He describes several of the characters, noting that Trollope seems to like people "on the verge of the outlaw class." He discusses book-reviewers as he feels they really are, and as Lady Carbury finds them, and feels that the corruption that does exist in the real reviewing world, though not as widespread as Lady Carbury's, is ample argument for an anonymous press.

137. Unsigned. "Recent Novels," London *Times*, 24 August, 1875, p. 4.

Review of *The Way We Live Now*. The reviewer notes, with a tone of regret, that this is a good novel: it is "only too faithful a portraiture of the manners and customs of the English at the latter part of this 19th century. . . . It is a likeness of the face which society wears today." He praises the fairness and powers of description evidenced in Trollope's presentation of both Melmotte and Felix Carbury; the characters are complex and understandable. Lady Carbury is described as a "splendid" achievement; no other author, this reviewer feels, could dare to ask our sympathy for such a woman. This is pronounced one of Trollope's very best works; the reviewer hopes that it will accomplish good by leading the readers to examine their own motives and those of their society.

138. Unsigned. "Editor's Table," *Appleton's Journal of Popular Literature, Science, and Art*, 14 (August, 28, 1875), 277-278.

Review of *The Way We Live Now*. The reviewer begins by remarking on the great number and great similarity of Trollope's "last half-dozen" novels, an indication that the author has put little effort into their writing, he feels. Then he adds, "Now we do not mean to intimate by this that we think poorly of Mr. Trollope's novels . . . few novels of our day are better in any respect than his, and none are more uniformly readable and amusing." He notes that this novel is a satire, and that probably never have a "more despicable set of people, actuated by meaner motives, and performing worse actions" been together in any one novel. The reviewer finds fault with the book, in that there is "no elevated standard" offered the reader among the characters. The reviewer also criticizes Trollope's jibes at editors and literary critics, and suggests that Trollope should take issue with his own illustrators, who do not do justice to this very superior novel.

139. Unsigned. Untitled, *Literary World*, 6 (September, 1875), 47.

Review of *The Way We Live Now*. This writer jokes that this will prove a very economical book, as its size will make the reading of it "last all summer." He does find it somewhat too long, and tedious in places; furthermore, he finds "no good lessons in it, no exemplary characters." The men he considers "brainless," and the women "adventurers." He then outlines the plot, labeling Lady Carbury "a monstrosity." In sum, he dismisses the novel as "coarse, dull, and dreary."

140. Unsigned. "Contemporary Literature: Belles Lettres," *Westminster Review*, American Edition, 104 (October, 1875), 257.

Review of *The Way We Live Now*. This writer suggests that all novelists should read this book, "if only for the sake of Lady Carbury," who is amazingly true to life. He sketches the plot as it surrounds her, and proceeds to note some similarities in character between Trollope himself and Lady Carbury. Trollope too writes "flabby sentences," especially when compared to Thackeray's "terse epigrams." He feels that Trollope "has taken a good subject, and made it fairly interesting, but nothing more." He complains that there is no "nobleness of character" in this work.

141. Unsigned. "Our Library Table," *Athenaeum*, no. 2512 (18 December, 1875), 829.

Review of *The Prime Minister*, part I (of 8). The reviewer anticipates from the segment of the novel already published that the remainder will be very good. He sketches the characters briefly.

142. Unsigned. Untitled, *Literary World*, 7 (June, 1876), 9.

Review of *The Prime Minister*. There is no question about this reviewers's opinion: "We think this novel is the most tedious that the author has ever perpetrated." He finds particular fault with the characters; there is "not a pleasant character in the book." The Wharton-Lopez plot is briefly summarized in conclusion.

143. [Collyer]. "Novels of the Week," *Athenaeum*, no. 2540 (1 July, 1876), 15.

Review of *The Prime Minister*. This reviewer finds the novel an unsuccessful attempt to combine two stories, that of the Duke of Omnium, and that centering on the "young lady who is blessed, or cursed, with two lovers." The reviewer praises the Wharton-Lopez story as a very good one, but can feel only a "languid interest" in the political plot. He insists that this is a domestic novel "with gratuitous political intrusions." However, he finds it does have some "clever scenes," and it is a better novel than *The Way We Live Now*.

144. Unsigned. "Recent Novels," London *Times,* 18 August, 1876, p. 4.

    Review of *The Prime Minister*. The reviewer begins with comments on the reappearance and growth of the characters of Trollope as a sure sign of his ability as a writer. He comments on Plantagenet Palliser's development through his novels from a cold and unlikeable person to a very sympathetic man. He recalls the growth through marriage of both Plantagenet and his wife Glencora, in contrast to the results of the wrong choice which Emily Wharton made in marrying Lopez. The descriptions of the politicians and of Lopez are praised; they help to balance the rest of the novel, which he declares is too predictable.

145. Unsigned. "The Prime Minister," *Saturday Review,* 42 (14 October, 1876), 481-482.

    This is a rather harsh review: "If the events . . . were true, they might possibly be interesting." But, this reviewer finds, the narrative is almost impossible to endure in fiction. He asserts that Emily Wharton is terribly stupid, Arthur Fletcher too full of "parochial virtues," and Mr. Wharton too credulous, to be accepted by the reader. He suggests that modern fiction has reached its limits, with George Eliot loading her work with abstruse ideas, and Trollope having no clear idea at all. Trollope's skill at copying has been praised but, this reviewer notes, that appeals only to a "certain class of minds," those who are unable to understand anything more complex. This story is finally vulgar, he finds, and the two plots never do coalesce. He outlines the story briefly, and finds it of no interest, except perhaps to the very dull.

146. Unsigned. "Editor's Table," *Appleton's Journal*, 2, n.s. (February, 1877), 187.

This article is suggested by the fact that Trollope recently gave a lecture at the School of Art in east London "on the rather hackneyed subject of reading." Trollope reportedly described reading as a valuable recreation, which this writer finds very admirable. He comments on the regrettably sensational tastes of young working people, and suggests that they need more information and direction toward good and enriching reading, and there are not many sources of these things. He commends Trollope for attempting to raise the level of taste of these young people.

147. [Collyer]. "Novels of the Week," *Athenaeum*, no. 2590 (16 June, 1877), 765-767.

Review of *The American Senator*. This reviewer calls the novel misnamed, as the title figure could be removed without changing or hurting the story. He declares that the senator's actions are fine, but when Trollope "uses him . . . to hang speeches on," he is very boring. The setting is praised as charming, due to the minuteness of description and the delicate humor which Trollope masters. The first chapter is mentioned as especially well written. The characters, while they have new names, are not very original; all in all, he finds this "not one of Mr. Trollope's best books."

148. Unsigned. "The American Senator," *Saturday Review*, 43 (30 June, 1877), 803-804.

The novel is criticized as "by no means one of the best" of Trollope's novels, but is admitted as above average. The reviewer notes Trollope's virtues as an ability to understand young people and particularly women. He outlines the Trefoil and Masters plots, noting that Senator Gotobed has very little importance in the novel; it would be quite as good if he were omitted altogether. On the whole, the reviewer concludes, this is pleasant reading.

149. Unsigned. "Recent Novels," London *Times*, 10 August, 1877, p. 3.

Review of *The American Senator*. The *Times* writer discusses briefly the "regularity" of Trollope's novels — referring both to their production and to their quality. On the average he finds they have a dependable "fair quality." He feels Trollope repeats the theme of one young woman with two suitors quite often, which tends to produce monotony. In the novel the same story line appears, but it is pleasantly told. The Senator, he finds, has "nothing to do with the actual double story" and proves nothing except his inability to understand "our institutions." The English come off well for hospitality, he thinks, in that they are unfailingly polite to the American boor. The Trefoil plot he describes as "exciting," and Mary Masters is an admirable figure.

150. Unsigned. "Books of the Day," *Appleton's Journal*, 3, n.s. (September, 1877), 288.

Review of *The American Senator*. The writer for *Appleton's* considers Trollope good summer reading, as his novels are long and placid, appropriate to the days and weather. He finds the novels very similar, with two or three exceptions; most of them resemble a "milk and water diet." *The American Senator* is among these, and will do just as well as another. The reviewer finds the figure of the senator to be "exaggerated," the story line "thin," and containing too much "smooth small-talk."

151. Shand, Alexander. "Mr. Anthony Trollope's Novels," *Edinburgh Review*, 146 (October, 1877), 455-488.

This is an extended essay on Trollope's books and life. Shand finds one major shortcoming in Trollope's works — a lack of depth — but declares that at what he does, Trollope is unsurpassed. He mentions that of all the novels Trollope has written, there have been only two disasters — *Miss Mackenzie* and *The Way We Live Now*. A good deal of Trollope's success is due to growth and development of characters who reappear in several novels; they become more real with each appearance. "Realism slightly idealized is his guiding law; yet the imagination must play no insignificant part in it." He notes that dialogue is the heart of the novels and Trollope's skill at transcribing dialogue is one of the causes of his popular success. Trollope's insistance on hospitality, if not intellect, in his heroes, and his vivid presentation of hunting are important to all the novels. Shand discusses a number of the novels and characters in some detail, though his judgments are rather general.

152. Unsigned. Untitled, *Literary World*, 8 (October, 1877), 74.

Review of *The American Senator*. This reviewer is not pleased: "Mr. Trollope is at his old task, the attempted cure by ridicule of the faults and follies of upper society life." He finds in this novel "the same sort of people" as appeared in *The Last Chronicle of Barset* and *The Way We Live Now*; none of these characters is either attractive or believeable. This reviewer also objects to the odd names Trollope gives his characters.

153. Morley, Henry. "Recent Literature," *Nineteenth Century*, 3 (February, 1878), 401.

The American Senator is included in a list of "recommended fiction."

126. [Collyer]. "Literature," *Athenaeum*, no. 2625 (16 February, 1878), 211-212.

Review of *South Africa*. The reviewer notes that Trollope's trip to Africa was hurried and that this rush is apparent in the book, which is nonetheless "entertaining and instructive." He cites a lack of excitement or great adventure in this travel book: "the narrative flows as smoothly as the incidents in a well-bred novel." The reviewer takes issue with some of Trollope's criticism of English policy in Africa as speculations of a traveller not familiar with all the facts; however, he agrees with some of Trollope's harsh judgments on the English missionaries. He finds the book valuable, though less complete than might be wanted.

155. Unsigned. "Trollope's South Africa." *Saturday Review*, 45 (23 February, 1878), 241-243.

The reviewer thinks it is very fortunate that Trollope wrote this book, as all British citizens must feel some interest in the area due to the recent sending of British troops there. He approves the work, for "in his two volumes on so very dull a subject as South Africa there is scarcely a dull page." The reviewer then gives an account of Trollope's observations on the responsibility of Great Britain to the African people, and recounts some of the personal adventures related by Trollope.

156. Unsigned. "Trollope's South Africa," London *Times*, 18 April, 1878, p. 7.

This reader finds Trollope's work an outstanding job of firsthand reporting in easily readable form. Because most British people cannot travel to Africa and cannot read through all the government-issued "blue books" on the topic, this is a very valuable work. The review contains a summary of the topics Trollope deals with, his accounts of his difficulties on the trip, and the political situations, population figures, and the like.

157. Unsigned. "Reviews," *Pall Mall Gazette*, 27 (2 May, 1878), 1656.

Review of *Is He Popenjoy*? The review begins with a description of the plot of the novel, and the observation that Mr. Trollope's style and presentation are very plain, especially in contrast to the writing of Mr. Wilkie Collins. He comments that Trollope is "frequently dull, but he is never untrue or unnatural." The reviewer consiers Trollope skillful even when he is not interesting; this is a simple story, told with a photographic truth to detail. This quality, the writer feels, endears Trollope to foreigners, and will make him invaluable to readers in the 20th century. Like some other writers, Trollope often shows a "want of tact" in his selection of characters' names — Miss Tallowax and Dr. Fleabody are especially noted, with the observation that Thackeray never commits such faults.

158. [Collyer]. "Novels of the Week," *Athenaeum*, 2636 (4 May, 1878), 567.

Review of *Is He Popenjoy*? This review, which seems to assume that the audience is familiar with the novel, describes chiefly the characters. The reviewer considers that Mary's feelings are "well-managed" by Trollope, but "[while] the elder marchioness is good at first the promise is not verified." He concludes the brief notice, "on the whole, there is much that is readable in the book."

159. Unsigned. "Is He Popenjoy?" *Saturday Review*, 45 (1 June, 1878), 695-696.

The reviewer begins by noting that fiction must be reticent on certain points, and that "vice must wear a veil, however thin." The reviewer then rather abruptly turns to a specific discussion of this new novel, noting that the characters are rather like those in the Barchester series, except that Trollope does not seem to like them so well. He sketches the plot of the novel, noting the unattractiveness of Lord George, and proceeds to remark that Trollope seems to think men in general are easy prey for any designing woman. This novel, he feels, shows a decline in Trollope's powers.

160. Unsigned. "The Novels of Anthony Trollope," *Literary World,* 9 (July, 1878), 28-29.

Here is a brief article asserting that some novels, including Trollope's, "present fiction in form and color which distort the truth and push satires to an extravagance which degrades them into lampoons." But a recent legal case in Ireland, regarding the Bagot will, seems to prove that Trollope is not so unrealistic after all, and the writer promises to believe what Trollope says about the behavior of the English people in the future.

161. Unsigned. "The South African Question," *Blackwood's Edinburgh Magazine,* 124 (July, 1878), 97-118.

This is an article about South Africa; Trollope's book is cited as one of the authorities the writer consulted. He summarizes Trollope's book as "very pleasant" and written in a "most pleasant vein," and remarks on the great amount of information which Trollope obtained first-hand about Africa. The author of this article takes a patronizing attitude toward the African natives, and refers to anecdotes or statistics from Trollope's work to support his opinions.

162. Unsigned. Untitled, *Literary World,* 9 (July, 1878), 30.

Review of *Is He Popenjoy?* The attractive format of this publication draws the reviewer's first notice; he proceeds to the judgment that the content is first rate as well: this is "one of the strongest" of Trollope's works. Trollope is praised for holding "a mirror up to nature," as the plot is outlined. The reviewer finds occasionally some coarseness in the descriptions, though this is not a major flaw.

163. Unsigned. "The Lady of Launay," *Literary World,* 9 (September, 1878), 56.

This brief notice describes the story as "very clever and pretty." The reviewer sketches the plot and notes that it is simple but endearing.

164. Unsigned. "Is He Popenjoy?" London *Times,* 14 September, 1878, p. 4.

The reviewer judges this novel a "moderate performance" by Trollope, not really worthy of him. He suggests that it was written hastily and carelessly, noting the "senselessness" of the names as one evidence. He briefly describes the plot and objects to it as vulgar and disagreeable. Adelaide Houghton, he feels, belongs in a French novel, but certainly not in one by Anthony Trollope. He finds the women's rights sub-plot altogether unnecessary.

165. Escott, T. H. S. "A Novelist of the Day," *Time: a Monthly Miscellany of Interesting and Amusing Literature,* 1 (1879), 626-632.

Escott writes an extended and laudatory general review of the novels of Trollope. He specifically mentions *The Warden, Barchester Towers, Orley Farm,* and *The Three Clerks* as outstanding. Trollope has a drive to carry out a theme which occasionally tramples factual realism, Escott feels; but Trollope, while an enthusiast in his social criticism, is also a practical man. He notes the careful details of Irish life in the Irish novels, and the touches of Salisbury in the Barchester series. He concludes with a biography of the novelist.

166. [Collyer]. "Reviews," *Athenaeum*, 2672 (11 January, 1879), 47.

Review of *An Eye For An Eye*. The reviewer disparages the story as "slight," but contends that Trollope has made it interesting because of his art as a narrator. He finds a compelling moral lesson in the story: "The tragedy on the cliffs at Ardmore is intended to mark the dire lapse from honour to which mere affectionate selfishness may lead an ordinary man."

167. Unsigned. "On Novel Reading," *Literary World*, 10 (February, 1879), 40.

This article is written in response to an article by Trollope, "Novel-reading: The Works of Charles Dickens; the Works of W. Makepeace Thackeray," which appeared in the January issue of *Nineteenth Century* [See below, entry T63]. First, the writer summarizes Trollope's article, then commends the treatment of the authors mentioned in that article: "We heartily agree with him that the highest function of the novel is to teach the great truths and duties that underlie good living."

168. Unsigned. "An Eye for an Eye," *Literary World*, 10 (February, 1879), 53.

The novel in question is described as "tragic," and quite as interesting as the longer works of its author. It can be read, this reviewer feels, as a sermon on the text, "the wages of sin is death." He remarks further, "As in everything he writes, Mr. Trollope's purpose here is to show the heartlessness of much of the English pride of family and name," and concludes that "its subject is one that ought to forbid its indiscriminate circulation."

169. Unsigned. "Contemporary Literature. IV. Novelists," *Blackwood's Edinburgh Magazine*, 125 (March, 1879), 322-344.

This article seems addressed to potential writers of novels. It discusses novel-writing in general, the more practical motivations of men as opposed to women writers, and proceeds to offer comments and advice on such elements as style, use of cliches, structures of plots, etc. Mention is made of a number of contemporary novelists. About Trollope, the writer says he is "more distinctly the family novelist than any man who has gone before him." This fame is, he feels, deserved, although Trollope sometimes slips in quality and introduces extraneous and/or unedifying characters and incidents into his stories. Trollope is described as the "confidant of well-regulated love affairs and the realistic painter of middle-class life."

170. Unsigned. "Reviews," *Saturday Review,* 47 (29 March, 1879), 410-411.

Review of *An Eye for an Eye.* This reviewer thinks that Trollope's later works have seemed machine-made; he fails because his heart and soul are not longer evident in his work. The "religious woman" who keeps repeating the title phrase seems only half-convincing to this reviewer. The plot is summarized, and the characterization of Father Marty is praised. He concludes: "We may congratulate the author on the moral of the story."

171. Unsigned. "Anthony Trollope's Writings," *Literary World,* 10 (June, 1879), 189.

Here, without comment, is a list of Trollope's published works, in chronological order, with the dates of publication.

172. [Collyer?]. "Literature," *Athenaeum,* 2694 (14 June, 1879), 749-750.

Review of *English Men of Letters — Thackeray.* The reviewer notes that this book is rather disappointing in that it does not contain "complete" information about one of the most outstanding men of the century. But, he adds, it is well known that Thackeray had requested that no private details of his life be published, and his family had enforced this request. Trollope's book is praised as being the "most truthful and complete likeness" possible under the circumstances. Collyer notes that the eulogy is not elaborate nor over-done, and summarizes the book as an argument that Thackeray was not the cynic that many people supposed.

173. [Sergeant]. "Novels of the Week," *Athenaeum*, 2694 (14 June, 1879), 755.

Review of *John Caldigate*. This writer finds the present book similar to *Barchester Towers,* for the "racy" quality of its "turns of expression and illustrations." He quotes a description of a woman bringing "grub" to the table and "chucking" it down so as to splatter. He praises Trollope's mastery of presenting conversation; then, rather surprisingly, he concludes that *John Caldigate* is interesting, but "its art is neither specially elaborate nor very well sustained."

174. [Wise, J. R.] "Contemporary Literature," *Westminster Review*, 112 (July, 1879), 125.

Review of *English Men of Letters – Thackeray*. This short, one-paragraph review describes the biography as true, but calls the critical judgments "capricious."

175. Unsigned. "John Caldigate," *Literary World*, 10 (August, 1879), 259-60.

This novel, the reviewer feels, like *Is He Popenjoy?* is characterized by a "minute survey of the field of action," a "background of disreputable conduct," the slow "evolution of a happy issue with the discomfiture of all rascals concerned."

In this way, it is quite different from *Orley Farm, Framley Parsonage,* and *The Last Chronicle of Barset.* This is so different, the reviewer thinks, that one might not recognize it as the work of Trollope. He outlines the plot, noting an error in the description of courtroom procedures. He concludes that as a study of character the book is worth while, adding that it is thus far "the novel of the season" in general conversation.

176. Unsigned. "Thackeray," *Literary World,* 10 (August, 1879), 279.

This biography of Trollope's friend is in the reviewer's opinion, the most readable in the series of biographies directed by Morley. The reviewer does wish that Trollope had known Thackeray longer and more intimately, so that he could have written a more thorough account of his life, and could have been freer to write "more warmly."

177. Unsigned. "Recent Novels," London *Times,* 8 August, 1879, p. 3.

Review of *John Caldigate.* This reviewer summarizes the plot of the novel and comments that it is "a good novel expanded into a dull one," and that several of the characters are too gloomy to be interesting.

178. Unsigned. "John Caldigate," *Saturday Review,* 48 (16 August, 1879), 216-217.

The reviewer notes that bigamy has become a popular topic for novels, and in this one Mr. Trollope uses it. Moreoever, "we regret that his powers ashould have been expended on a theme which can scarcely be touched with a free hand without awakening sympathies in a wrong direction." He notes that Trollope often creates idealized women, while his men (even the heroes) are easily led astray, as John Calidgate is here. The reviewer sketches the principal characters and the plot, asserting that the real hero is Samuel Bagwax. He remarks that all of Trollope's good features are here — humor, close observation, and the like. He objects to Trollope's treatment of Mrs. Bolton as too severe. He trusts that Trollope will choose a more wholesome theme for his next novel.

179. Unsigned. "Novels of the Week," *Athenaeum*, 2712 (18 October, 1879), 495.

Review of *Cousin Henry*. This is a very brief review, chiefly negative. The minuteness of description is praised, while the story as a whole is dismissed as "so much ado about nothing."

180. Unsigned. "Reviews," *Pall Mall Gazette,* 30 (18 October, 1879), 1336.

Review of the *Life of Thackeray*. The reviewer opens by remarking that Morley made a very poor choice for this volume in the "Men of Letters" series, noting that Trollope's book needs much correction in "grammar and style." He feels the "praise is so conventional and undiscriminating as to raise a doubt whether the author appreciates his subject," and the criticism is both unfair and verbose. He thinks Trollope pays too much attention to Thackeray's financial affairs, and unjustly faults Thackeray for not writing more regularly, as he himself did. He also accuses Trollope of being in error in some of the "facts" asserted about Thackeray. The reviewer thinks that Trollope is not capable of appreciating an author like Thackeray, and "It follows that we ought not to blame Mr. Trollope, but rather regret for his own sake that such a task as this was given to him."

181. Unsigned. "Cousin Henry," *Saturday Review,* 48 (25 October, 1879), 515-516.

The reviewer remarks, "this is not a novel exactly, but rather a study, and a very able one." He feels that the story is an attack on conscience. The plot is summarized, with observations on the manipulation of the reader's sympathies. He notes that "daring villains are now a popular subject of novels," and Trollope has handled this one well.

182. Unsigned. "Recent Novels," London *Times,* 6 November, 1879, p. 6.

Review of *Cousin Henry.* This writer terms the novel a "clever study of a weak and vicious man, but not a satisfying novel." He summarizes the plot and repeats his objections to the hero.

183. Unsigned. "Current Fiction," *Literary World,* 11 (14 February, 1880), 58.

Review of *Cousin Henry.* Trollope's skill in writing fiction so believable that it seems more like history is praised here. The plot of this novel is briefly sketched.

184. Unsigned. "News and Notes," *Literary World,* 11 (28 February, 1880), 80.

This is a brief item in a column, to the effect that Trollope is now 65 years old, and is much more attractive in person than the popular portrait of him would indicate.

185. [Cook]. "Novels of the Week," *Athenaeum,* 2744 (29 May, 1880), 694-695.

Review of *The Duke's Children.* The return of familiar characters is welcomed by this critic, who notes that they have realistically aged since their last appearance. He condemns those who disparage Trollope for not leading his readers "to see the beauties of a higher life," and asserts that they have missed the point; Trollope "takes life as he sees it . . . . He has no esoteric doctrines. His lessons are plain to all the world." This reviewer declines to summarize the plot, as that might spoil the readers' pleasure in it; he comments on the delights of Trollope's playfulness and the excellence of his narration.

186. Unsigned. "The Duke's Children," *Saturday Review,* 49 (12 June, 1880), 767-768.

This reviewer recounts Trollope's account of the composition of *Framley Parsonage* in his Thackeray biography, and remarks on the capacity of discipline to carry one through non-inspired times. He declares that three of the characters of *The Duke's Children* are successfully drawn – Plantagenet Palliser, Lady Mabel, and Isabel Boncassin. He notes that the individualized styles of speaking are what makes them outstanding characters. He offers a sketch of the plot, and notes that the Duke deserves sympathy, as he is so much better than his children.

187. Unsigned. Untitled, *Literary World,* 11 (31 July, 1880), 255.

Review of *The Duke's Children.* The reviewer admits that he enjoys Trollope's novels, and notes that familiarity with the kinds of problems, setbacks, and resolutions Trollope uses adds pleasure to the anticipation of each new novel. He then sketches the characters and crises of this novel; he deems the political episodes as "tedious," and chides the author for using the verb "got" instead of "have", but concludes that "of course *The Duke's Children* is worth reading."

188. Unsigned. "Anthony Trollope's Novels," *Literary World*, 11 (31 July, 1880), 266.

This article is a brief note indicating the order in which to read Trollope's novels: *The Warden, Barchester Towers, Dr. Thorne, Small House at Allington, Can You Forgive Her? The Last Chronicle of Barset, The Eustace Diamonds, Phineas Redux, The Prime Minister, The Duke's Children,* in that order, comprise the list given.

189. Unsigned. "Recent Literature," *Nineteenth Century*, 8 (August, 1880), 313-340.

Reviews of *The Duke's Children* and *John Caldigate*, and a number of other works. Of *The Duke's Children,* the reviewer notes that "we shall find many old acquaintances here." He remarks that the Duke's story is "humorously pathetic," and that Lady Mabel stands out as the best of these well-drawn characters. The reviewer is glad to see politics is "less prominent" in this work. *John Caldigate* is considered a credit to Trollope's versatility as a novelist, as it is quite difference from *The Duke's Children.* The most distinctive feature of this work is the character of John's wife, because of her courage, sweetness, and strength.

190. [Sedgwick, A. G.] "Mr. Trollope's Last Novel," *The Nation*, 31 (August 10, 1880), 138-139).

Review of *The Duke's Children.* Sedgwick's discussion is prompted by a recent critical review by Richard G. White, which unfavorably compared Trollope to Scott. Sedgwick notes that this age is more realistic in its tastes than was Scott's, and it is only natural that plot is now more important than character in fiction. Sedgwick feels such comparisons as White's are pointless. He then summarizes the plot of *The Duke's Children,* and declares it "one of Mr. Trollope's most successful books."

He regards Trollope as a master of narration, with the skill to make his writing appear artless. He feels that Thackeray, Dickens, and George Eliot could all be edited to good effect, but not Trollope. Trollope is, he feels, analogous to Zola in some ways, but is not a "naturalist" in the French manner. Sedgwick concludes that Trollope is perhaps the "last of the realists," whose virtue as a storyteller is evident in readers always wanting to read more of him.

191. "Reviews," *Pall Mall Gazette,* 32 (12 August, 1880), 584.

Review of *The Duke's Children.* Too many novelists are, in this reviewer's opinion, producing fiction "by recipe," almost mechanically. He notes that Trollope recently explained that he "puts the cart before the horse," and that readers love this device, in great part because it is unlike what other novelists do. The reviewer notes that Trollope has written more, and more wholesome, entertainment than most authors, but he never suspected that so much of his popularity was due "to this habit of inverting the natural order of the narrative of his chronicles." In this latest story, one of the delights is the reappearance of familiar characters. Few of the new characters are to the reviewer's taste, especially Major Tifto and Lady Mabel Grex; even the Palliser children are "not entirely satisfactory." Mr. Tregear he finds "a calculating prig." Many of the characters, however, are "good fun," especially Lord Chiltern and Lord Cantripp. He sketches in some detail a number of the characters, concentrating on Lord Silverbridge.

192. Unsigned. "Contemporary Literature: Belles Lettres," *Westminster Review,* American ed., 114. (October, 1880), 278.

Review of *The Duke's Children.* This one-paragraph review declares that this new work offers proof that Trollope's writing powers are not "falling off." This novel shows "all the ease of his best days."

193. Unsigned. "Novels of the Week," *Athenaeum*, 2777 (January, 1881), 93.

Review of *Dr. Wortle's School*. The reviewer praises the shorter than usual length of this Trollope novel, and finds noteworthy the "novelty in method" of narration. He sketches the plot briefly, and declares that it is told "with much skill and a good deal of quiet pathos and humour."

194. Unsigned. "Mr. Trollope's Cicero," *Pall Mall Gazette*, 33 (10 January, 1881), 123-124.

Review of *Life of Cicero*. Trollope is to be commended, this writer feels, on having done the immense amount of work to prepare this work. The reviewer knows that it was a "labor of love," as Trollope has always been very interested in Cicero and in his times, as well as in modern political life. He notes that the language of this biography is "easy and familiar" — perhaps not scholarly enough at times: "The great fault of the book . . . is the deficiency of nice scholarship." The reviewer chides the author for at least two "serious mistranslations," and explains the errors. He feels that nonetheless, on the whole, this is a contribution to the understanding of Cicero; Trollope has been more fair than some other historians, and has argued with reason against the common belief that Cicero was unmanly in his impatience and insincere in his public statements.

195. Unsigned. "Dr. Wortle's School," *Saturday Review*, 51 (22 January, 1881), 121-122.

Trollope has used very similar ingredients in previous novels, this writer notes, but they are his own and not borrowed. The story is certainly not stale. "The end is not good, and seems somewhat huddled-up; but the story goes off with great spirit." He briefly outlines the plot and notes that the telling, rather than the tale itself, is the main interest here. His only criticism is the insufficiently developed love affair between Lord Carstairs and Mary Wortle.

196. Unsigned. "Trollope's Life of Cicero," *Blackwood's Edinburgh Magazine,* 129 (February, 1881), 211-228.

The reviewer notes this is a very welcome book for those who do not read Latin. He quotes at some length from the volume to explain Trollope's motive in writing it, and sympathizes with Trollope for all the difficulties in attempting a fair biography of one so famous. He offers a synopsis of the work and comments that Trollope's admiration for his subject has colored the accounts of some incidents. He quotes several extended passages from the work.

197. Unsigned. "Trollope's Life of Cicero," *Saturday Review,* 51 (26 February, 1881), 279-280.

This reviewer states that, while the book is for the most part competently written, it does not deserve high praise. He considers that there were before now an ample number of books on Cicero; further, he notes that it is not a scholarly account, and Trollope did not take adequate notice of previous research. Trollope's inability to read German, he says, hampers this work. He finds carelessness and inexactness in several places, and feels Trollope exaggerates Cicero's virtues. Although the writing is, in places, "spritely," the reviewer finds it on the whole a superfluous and unbalanced book.

198. [Wise, J. R.] "Contemporary Literature," *Westminster Review,* 115 (April, 1881), 291-292.

Review of *Life of Cicero.* Trollope's narration of this work is described as informal and personal and filled with his deep admiration of and sympathy for Cicero. Wise comments that

Trollope does a service by revealing the humanity of Cicero to the modern reader.

199. Unsigned. Untitled, *Literary World*, 12 (9 April, 1881), 129-130.

Review of *Life of Cicero*. The reviewer begins by noting that this treatment of the Roman differs markedly from that of Mr. Froude, who sharply criticized Cicero in his book on Caesar. The reviewer outlines the book, and judges that Trollope is fair and scholarly, and more careful in his assessments than many historians. He concludes with favorable remarks on the indices and appendices, and indicates that this would be a valuable addition to any library.

200. Unsigned. "Recent Novels," London *Times*, 16 April, 1881, p. 10.

Review of *Dr. Wortle's School*. The reviewer begins by stating that this novel by Trollope first appeared anonymously in *Blackwood's Magazine*. He describes it as "strictly a novelette of character," and one of the most successful of Trollope's characterizations. He concludes with a brief plot summary.

201. Unsigned. "Novels of the Week," *Athenaeum*, 2795 (21 May, 1881), 686.

Review of *Ayala's Angel*. This critic mentions that all the characters in this novel are new, which indicates to him that the Palliser series is completed. He explains the title of the work, and comments on the troubles that money causes. He finds the book satisfactory for leisurely readers, but, in plot and interest, not comparable with Trollope's best.

202. "Reviews," *Pall Mall Gazette*, 33 (28 May, 1881), 2059-2060.

Review of *Ayala's Angel*. There are two major faults here, the reviewer announces: the first is that the heroine "is irresistably suggestive of champagne to the profane mind (he has forgotten some worthy vintages)"; and the second is that Trollope has used as the name of a Cornish house what is in fact the name of a real country house – Tregorthnan – which belongs to a living lord – Falmouth. Nonetheless, the reviewer feels, Trollope has "not written a better or pleasanter novel" for many years. There is not much plot here, he thinks, but that is outweighed by the wonderful characters. The reviewer then sketches the story, emphasizing the various characters.

203. Unsigned. "Ayala's Angel," *Saturday Review*, 51 (11 June, 1881), 756-757.

The reviewer notes that the title suggests a very exotic tale, but that this novel is in fact very English. He summarizes the story, finding fault with the heroine: she has "no real decision of character." He thinks the Colonel, however, is masterly, comparable to Thackeray's Dobbin. He especially admires Trollope's facility in presenting dialogue.

204. Unsigned. "Contemporary Literature," *Westminster Review*, 116 (July, 1881), 137.

Review of *Dr. Wortle's School*. In this novel, the reviewer states, Trollope seems to allow the story to develop as it goes along, rather than to have a pre-planned plot. He feels Trollope is comparable to Balzac for "real human interest," though Trollope is not so profound a thinker as the French writer. He concludes that Trollope deserves praise for his ability to make the reader take an interest in such characters as appear here.

205. Unsigned. "Recent Novels," London *Times*, 16 July, 1881, p. 5.

Review of *Ayala's Angel*. This novel is termed "one of the most lively and readable" of Trollope's works, although it is far from his best. The chief faults which the reviewer finds are its secular tone, a lack of thoughtful characters, and the presence of unnecessary characters and incidents. He concludes with a brief plot synopsis.

206. Unsigned. "Literature," *Athenaeum*, 2806 (6 August, 1881), 170-172.

Review of *The Life of Cicero*. This critic notes the large number of works already written on Cicero, citing Abeken, Watson, and Tyrrell as prominent. Judging this work to be "well written," the critic quotes a number of passages as illustrations. He notes that Trollope has disproved some common assumptions about the character of Cicero and cites a few minor errors in fact or date in Trollope's book, although he generally approves the scholarship of the biography.

207. Unsigned. Untitled, *Literary World*, 12 (27 August, 1881), 287-288.

Review of *Ayala's Angel* and *Dr. Wortle's School*. The review opens with an admission by the writer of a fondness for Trollope's novels and a recognition of their similarity to each other. He particularly enjoys the good humor, the sense of the ridiculous, and the mastery of characterization he finds in Trollope. *Dr. Wortle's School*, he comments, is slighter and shorter than Trollope usually produces; he sketches the basis of the plot. In *Ayala's Angel* he sees Trollope in full gear, "amusing," "saucy," and "audacious." There are a number of stock characters and situations, and the signs that Trollope has "written too much too fast" to be first rate. Americans in particular, he thinks, will find a "coarse vein" here.

208. Unsigned. "Contemporary Literature," *Westminster Review*,

118 (October, 1881), 287-288.

Review of *Ayala's Angel*. The *Westminster* reviewer sketches the plot of the novel and comments that those who enjoy Trollope will probably like this work, and perhaps even those who do not usually like him will enjoy it.

209. Unsigned. "Novels of the Week," *Athenaeum*, 2829 (14 January, 1882), 54.

Review of *Why Frau Frohmann Raised Her Prices, and Other Stories*. The reviewer lists the "other stories" in the volume: "The Lady of Launay," "Christmas at Thompson Hall," "The Telegraph Girl," and "Alice Dugdale." He summarizes two of these, and concludes that in the collection, "we see much of the author's skill and little of his occasional tameness."

210. Unsigned. "Frau Frohmann," *Saturday Review*, 53 (11 March, 1882), 305-306.

Review of *Why Frau Frohmann Raised Her Prices and Other Stories*. This reviewer finds the work a disappointing collection from Trollope. The stories are dismissed as "slight," and the book's binding as too fancy. He feels that professional novelists are finally faced with two alternatives: "either the invention must overstep bounds previously respected," or "it must repeat itself." Dickens he accuses of the first mistake, and Trollope of the second. He softens his final judgment somewhat, noting that Trollope's lesser works yet have more "flavour and spirit" than the best of many other authors.

211. Unsigned. "Novels of the Week," *Athenaeum*, 2837 (11 March, 1882), 314-315.

Review of *The Fixed Period*. The review consists of a plot summary with several passages quoted from the story. The reviewer's judgment is that this "amusing jeu d'esprit" is an agreeable diversion" from Trollope's usually contemporary settings and plots.

212. Unsigned. "Reviews," *Pall Mall Gazette*, 35 (14 March, 1882), 5.

Review of *The Fixed Period*. The reviewer notes that most authors feel compelled to write at least one fantasy, and this is Mr. Trollope's. He applauds the political meetings depicted in the story as among Trollope's best sketches, terming them "light and lively social descriptions, and pleasant samples of character." He feels the satire could be stronger, but that this is presumably an experiment for Trollope, who is usually a devout realist.

213. Unsigned. "The Fixed Period," *Saturday Review*, 53 (8 April, 1882), 434-435.

This writer notes that the novel appeared serially (in *Blackwood's*) and has aroused curiosity among readers as to its meaning. Many expected the story would conclude as a Swiftian political satire, but were disappointed that it did not come up to such expectations. He offers a plot summary, and notes that Great Britain, like the country in the tale, is ruled by old men. He asserts that a reader will "find a good deal to amuse, and something to puzzle him, in the motives and meanings that he may suspect to lie hidden." The reviewer, however, attempts only a partial explication: the story may be "a sort of epic intended to exhibit dogged obstinacy in heroic proportions."

214. Unsigned. "Recent Novels," London *Times*, 12 April, 1882, p. 3.

Review of *The Fixed Period*. This reviewer considers the story "essentially ghastly." He summarizes the plot and judges that it is impossible "to excite any very lively interest in the beings of a society as far removed from our actual experience as from our time." The few "lively scenes," he feels, do not redeem the book.

215. Untitled, *Literary World*, 13 (3 June, 1882), 189.

Review of *The Fixed Period, Why Frau Frohmann Raised Her Prices and Other Stories,* and *Marion Fay*. This reviewer says of *The Fixed Period* only that it "is meant to turn to an amusing account" the plan to expedite deaths of old people. Of the second volume, he feels that "Frau Frohmann" is a pointless story, apparently in an attempt to point out "a moral about the currency." Of the collection, he considers "The Telegraph Girl" and "Alice Dugdale" much superior, as they point out that marriage should be based on love rather than money. More reviewing space is devoted to *Marion Fay,* which is described as a "thorough-going Trollope novel." The plot is outlined, and described as "sad." Lord Hampton is the best of the characters, "a fine specimen of a man," as is the Welsh lord. The reviewer concludes that the novel is a "battery of guns slyly trained against aristocracy, rank, social pride, pretension, and emptiness."

216. Unsigned. "Mr. Trollope's New Novel," *Pall Mall Gazette,* 35 (22 June, 1882), 5.

Review of *Marion Fay*. The reviewer begins by noting the frequency of appearance of novels by Trollope, and suggests that they might be more individual if he wrote one every three years instead of two each year. He outlines the structure of the story, noting the familiarity of most of the elements. It is nonetheless, he feels, "agreeable reading," but has its faults: Lord Hampsted and Lady Frances are "very nearly ciphers;" Clare is "too common;" and Mr. Greenwood is "too lurid."

217. Unsigned. "Novels of the Week," *Athenaeum*, 2852 (24 June, 1882), 793-794.

Review of *Marion Fay*. The greater part of this review is a synopsis of the novel. The critic detects the faults he calls Trollope's usual ones here — overstatement and repetition; but he finds also some of the lightness of the early, first-rate stories.

218. Unsigned. "Contemporary Literature," *Westminster Review*, 118 (July, 1882), 138.

Review of *The Fixed Period*. The writer of this brief review outlines the plot of the novel and remarks that it is admirable for the skillful writing.

219. Unsigned. "Marian Fay," *Saturday Review*, 54 (8 July, 1882), 64-65.

This reviewer notes with some pleasure that Trollope here shows his old manner and topics. There are titled people in the leading roles, with the "democratic element fighting against the aristocratic." He notes that Trollope always seems to side theoretically with the democrats, but he does admire the finish of things aristocratic. He notes, rather disparagingly, that Trollope has piled into this novel all sorts of currently popular ideas — agnosticism, wicked clergy, and the like — and finds in this fact evidence of Trollope's "jaded fancy." He briefly sketches the plot, noting that Trollope here does not seem in total agreement with the man he makes the hero of the novel.

220. Unsigned. "Lord Palmerston," *Saturday Review*, 54 (5 August, 1882), 182-183.

This reviewer argues with Trollope's language and his judgments.

He notes that Trollope refers to Palmerston at one point as a "bully," and asserts that Russell was second only to Palmerston in capability as leader of the House; the reviewer objects to both of these claims. He cites inaccuracies due to Trollope's faulty memory and laziness in not checking things out carefully. He finds Trollope's judgment generally sound, with a few exceptions. He concludes the review with his own praise of Palmerston and his policies.

221. Unsigned. "Reviews," *Pall Mall Gazette*, 36 (25 August, 1882), 5.

Review of *Lord Palmerston*. Mr. Trollope shows his literary skill, this reviewer feels, by focussing on the crucial points in Palmerston's life, and by revealing that "he is not blind to his hero's faults . . ." He finds this book appealing for readers and notes that "There is something about Mr. Trollope's style . . . which invites confidence" in his conclusions. He concludes that here is an interesting and candid biography.

222. Unsigned. "Our Library Table," *Athenaeum*, 2864 (16 September, 1882), 367.

Review of *English Political Leaders – Lord Palmerston*. The reviewer declares that it was "not judicious" to ask Trollope, who is good at other things, to compile this biography. While Trollope's admiration and first-hand knowledge are worth something, this reviewer feels that his lack of precision and the obvious haste in writing are serious faults. This is "by no means a sufficient or satisfactory account of Palmerston as an English political leader."

223. Unsigned. "Contemporary Literature: History and Biography," *Westminster Review*, 118 (October, 1882), 273.

Review of *English Political Leaders – Lord Palmerston*. This brief notice includes a favorable comment on the discussion of foreign policy matters in the biography.

224. Unsigned. Untitled, *Pall Mall Gazette,* 36 (6 November, 1882), 9.

This is a brief note that Anthony Trollope suffered an attack on "Friday last" and four doctors were called in. This morning, Monday, "he seems much better."

225. Unsigned. Untitled, *Pall Mall Gazette,* 36 (8 November, 1882), 9.

This brief note declares that Mr. Trollope is "decidedly better" this morning.

226. Unsigned. Untitled, *Pall Mall Gazette,* 36 (9 November, 1882), 9.

A note indicates that Anthony Trollope is "much better" this morning.

227. Unsigned. "Novels of the Week," *Athenaeum,* 2873 (18 November, 1882), 658.

Review of *Kept in the Dark.* The reviewer describes this as a short work and "an amusing society story told in the well-known style" of Trollope. He summarizes the plot and comments on several of the characters, and almost parenthetically makes a note of Trollope's illness.

228. Unsigned. Untitled, *Pall Mall Gazette,* 36 (20 November, 1882), 9.

"Mr. Anthony Trollope is reported to be doing well."

229. Unsigned. Untitled, *Pall Mall Gazette,* 36 (21 November, 1882), 9.

"Mr. Anthony Trollope's progress towards recovery is also in every respect satisfactory."

230. Unsigned. Untitled, *Pall Mall Gazette,* 36 (29 November, 1882), 9.

This is a brief note: "Mr. Anthony Trollope has made considerable progress towards recovery during the past fortnight, but his general condition still gives rise to some anxiety."

231. Unsigned. Untitled, *Pall Mall Gazette,* 36 (2 December, 1882), 9.

This note quotes Trollope's doctor's bulletin to the effect that Trollope is losing strength, and remarks: "We regret to hear that Mr. Anthony Trollope is not so well."

232. Unsigned. "Anthony Trollope," London *Times,* 7 December, 1882, p. 6.

Obituary notice. The writer begins with a formal statement that Trollope died the previous day (December 6) after several weeks' illness. He gives an account of Trollope's life, noting his long years of work for the post office and his successful innovations there. The writer goes on to describe Trollope's writing as initially a distraction from his work for the Post Office, and notes the large number of volumes he produced and the wide popularity he gained from them. He describes Trollope's diligent work habits, noting that they resulted in novels that were "each very much the same throughout." He further describes the novels as "never over-deep or metaphysical," and "always entertaining." He ends on a positive note, saying that "[Trollope] has enriched our English fiction with characters destined to survive," mentioning that among these are Harry Hotspur, Mrs. Proudie, the Rev. Crawley, and the types of politicians, scamps, nouveau riches, and fine young women. The writer considers Trollope's "most perfect" novel to be *The Last Chronicle of Barset*.

233. Unsigned. "Death of Mr. Anthony Trollope," *Pall Mall Gazette*, 36 (7 December, 1882), 6.

   This obituary notice recounts Trollope's education, occupations, the course of his recent and fatal illness, and lists his publications.

234. Unsigned. Untitled, *Pall Mall Gazette*, 36 (7 December, 1882), 12.

   This article is a collection of quotations from leading daily journals regarding the death of Trollope on December 6. The papers quoted are the London *Times,* the *Morning Post,* the *Standard,* the *Daily News,* and the *Daily Chronicle.* All the articles quoted express regret at Trollope's death, and admiration for his writings.

235. Unsigned. "Anthony Trollope," *Saturday Review,* 54 (9 December, 1882), 755-756.

   Obituary notice. This writer praises Trollope as having touched great numbers of readers in a personal way. Trollope's keen observation and penetration, his ability to write so as to be easily understood, his knowledge of the workings of both feminine and masculine minds, were all remarkable. The writer of this notice classes him as a novelist equal to Jane Austen, Miss Ferrier, and Thackeray. He notices and denounces as stupid those critics who complained of Trollope as too prolific and/or a mechanical writer, and cites the enormous number and variety of characters he created. To those who say he could not write a tragedy, this writer offers *Nina Balatka* and *Linda Tressel* as rebuttals. Trollope the man deserves great praise, especially for his kindness to young and beginning writers.

236. Unsigned. "Obituary Notices," *Athenaeum*, 2876 (9 December, 1882), 772-773.

The *Athenaeum* writer begins with an appreciation and a biography of Trollope. He then sketches broadly the literary achievements of the man. "Mr. Trollope was at his best in kindly ridicule of the approved superficialities of life. His satire was rarely profound and his scorn seldom made deep gashes." The author feels that he was superior to both Dickens and Thackeray at "plot-making," primarily because he chose everyday subjects. Trollope's non-fiction he dismisses as showing "not much talent," but being occasionally interesting.

237. Unsigned. "Reviews," *Pall Mall Gazette*, 36 (9 December, 1882), 20.

Review of *Kept in the Dark*. The reviewer notes that Trollope wrote here about a pack of fools, and describes the main characters in verification of this judgment. He does remark that this is a "tolerably fresh treatment" of old Trollopian themes. He does not admire the heroine, Cecilia, and particularly objects to her addressing her husband as "my own, own man." He thinks Dick Ross could have played a larger part in the story, but finds the way in which the two "criminals" pay each other out entertaining.

238. Unsigned. "Funeral of Mr. Anthony Trollope," *Pall Mall Gazette*, 36 (11 December, 1882), 7.

This is a one-paragraph description of the funeral, which was held on December 9, and the burial in Kensal Green Cemetery.

It notes that the funeral was of a "private unostentatious character," and that only family members and very close friends were in attendance. The procession consisted of the "hearse, four mourning coaches, and three private carriages."

239. Unsigned. Untitled, *Knowledge, An Illustrated Magazine of Science* (15 December, 1882), 462.

The writer notes Trollope's death earlier in the month, "and for our part, we deem such a loss far more serious to the world than many others about which much more is said." The burden of the article is an attack on the "startling suggestion" in the *Times* article on Trollope that Mr. Crawley is a "development in recent times of the 'Mr. Collins' of Miss Austen's days! Could false criticism go much further than this!" The writer insists on the dissimilarity of the two characters: we "love" Mr. Crawley, while we feel something beneath "hatred" for Mr. Collins. He ends the paragraph, "But it angers one to think that the man who could draw as Trollope did here, should have left so many crude and imperfect sketches."

240. Unsigned. Untitled, *Literary World,* 13 (16 December, 1882), 456.

The writer of this obituary notice gives a brief biography of the novelist before his evaluation. He remarks that it is "no disparagement to say . . . he was not Dickens or Thackeray," although he was "in some respects the equal" of them. He mentions the kinds of "stock characters" which Trollope employed, but commends him for his sense of humor and his sense of values: "He has written nothing which will not help make truer hearts and better lives." He urges readers to read the novels of Trollope, and concludes with a list of them and their dates of publication.

241. Unsigned. Untitled, *Knowledge, An Illustrated Magazine of Science* (22 December, 1882), 475.

The writer here defends his previous article on Trollope which appeared in the same journal on December 15, 1882. "A contemporary takes us to task, though not unkindly, for saying that the death of a novelist is a more serious calamity than many about which more is said." His general line of defense is that most people do not genuinely miss kings or politicians, but "when a Thackerary dies, who can even complete his last unfinished work?" He does not specifically mention Trollope by name in this article.

242. Oliphant, Mrs. "Anthony Trollope," *Good Words*, 24 (1883), 142-144.

In this critical essay occasioned by Trollope's death, Mrs. Oliphant comments on her fellow-novelist's fame and accomplishments. He became, through his works, "an acquaintance of the world." He was not a philosopher, she says, as George Eliot was; nor was he a humorist as Thackeray was. She defends him as a "fair and sound historian of England," which none of the "greater" writers was. She predicts that "the best of Anthony Trollope will be inscribed in the historic and social annals of the country, and will show our great grandchildren many a characteristic picture of those days when Victoria was Queen." She recounts Trollope's contributions of stories to *Good Words*, and the rejection of one of them as "unsuitable" by Dr. McLeod, the editor. She concludes that Westminster Abbey, though not the grave of Trollope, contains many less noteworthy people; he "has been as much a faithful servant of England as if he had fought half a hundred battles."

243. Unsigned. "Anthony Trollope," *The Month: A Catholic Magazine and Review*, 49 (1883), 484.

Review of *An Autobiography*. The writer of this review clearly admires Trollope's work: "It is not too much to say that scarcely any English novelist has during his lifetime been more popular — and more deservedly popular — than Anthony Trollope." He points out that the novelist has given hours of interest and amusement to "the educated class of English novel-readers." The reviewer takes note of the enormous number of Trollope's publications, and his own account of the steady, regular writing which produced them. The reviewer then summarizes Trollope's account of his life, and suggests that the best novels Trollope wrote are *Framley Parsonage* and *The Small House at Allington,* rather than the novelist's favorite, *The Last Chronicle of Barset.* The reviewer concludes by predicting that Trollope's characters, for all their contemporary popularity, will not be remembered as long as will Jane Eyre, Mr. Rochester, Colonel Newcombe, Becky Sharp, Tito, and Romola.

244. Freeman, Edward A. "Anthony Trollope," *Macmillan's,* 47 (January, 1883), 236-240.

This is primarily a "remembrance" by a critic who knew Trollope for the last year or so of the latter's life. He comments on their disagreements about field sports, and their long conversations about ancient Rome and Cicero's part in it. He judges Trollope as superior to Dickens at characterization, and as less profound than George Eliot.

245. Unsigned. "Contemporary Literature: Belles Lettres," *Westminster Review,* 119 (January, 1883), 139.

Notice of *Kept in the Dark.* The writer merely mentions the book as recently published, and notes that Trollope has died.

246. Unsigned. "Recent Literature," *Manhattan: A Publication for Oddfellows,* 1 (January, 1883), 74.

Review of *Kept in the Dark*. The reviewer opens with a note of Trollope's recent death, and the judgment that "he was by no means a great artist, and of late his productions were becoming thin in quality," although over the years he has given much "innocent pleasure" in his novels. He describes the beginning of the story, but leaves the resolution of it for the reader to discover.

247. [Bryce, J.]. "English Fiction: the Death of Anthony Trollope," *The Nation*, 36 (January 4, 1883), 10-11.

Bryce praises Trollope as the highest in the "second rank" of authors, noting that the "first rank" contains Thackeray, Dickens, and George Eliot. Trollope is clearly above authors such as Miss Braddon, Mrs. Wood, Ouida, William Black, James Payn, Whyte, and Melville. Bryce declares that Trollope's creations are "a part of the common thought of cultivated Englishmen." He gives a brief outline of Trollope's life, and concludes that if Trollope is read in fifty years, it will be for the exact and accurate portrayal of everyday life in England under Victoria. Trollope's range of writing is not wide, but is surprisingly good nonetheless; each of his characters is clearly of a class and yet still a unique individual. Many of Trollope's contemporary novelists are writers of incident, and thus not memorable. Though Trollope has too many characters in his works, this flaw is redeemed by the brightness and faithfulness of his sketches.

248. Freeman, Edward A. "Anthony Trollope," *Living Age*, 156 (6 January, 1883), 177-178.

This is a reprint of the article that appeared in *Macmillans* (see above, entry 244).

249. Unsigned. "From Miss Austen to Mr. Trollope," *Living Age*, 156 (6 January, 1883), 186-189.

The recent republication of Jane Austen's works and the recent death of Anthony Trollope suggested to this writer a comparison of the two as novelists. He focusses on the clergy, the styles of life, the patterns of thought, depicted in their novels. He considers Anthony Trollope's work to be more of this world than Jane Austen's, though he thinks most readers will find her world more appealing. As an example, he points out that Trollope's characters live in and around London, and deal with the real pressures of that fact, while Jane Austen's characters hardly seem to know that London exists.

250. Unsigned. "A Note from England," *Literary World*, 14 (13 January, 1883), 8.

This writer, noting a number of recent deaths of prominent people, including Trollope, expresses the belief that many men work themselves to death. He thinks this very likely in the case of Trollope, who is rumored to have left 100,000£ at the time of his death. If this is true, the writer continues, it was very foolish: "For the man who kills himself by writing novels merely to heap thousands on thousands, it is difficult to find an apology. He had enough . . . years and years ago."

251. Unsigned. "World Biographies," *Literary World*, 14 (13 January, 1883), 9.

This article is a collection of quotations from obituary notices from the *Athenaeum*, the *Academy*, the *Saturday Review*, and the *Spectator*. They all express regret at Trollope's death and mention some of his best-known works.

252. Meetkerke, Cecilia E. "Anthony Trollope," *Blackwood's Edinburgh Magazine*, 133 (February, 1883), 316-320.

Ms. Meetkerke devotes most of this article to an expression of personal admiration for Trollope, the man, with anecdotes to illustrate his goodness and friendliness. She defends his literature as great despite its "ordinariness" of subject matter, and calls his novels the "acknowledged type of that blameless, entertaining, beneficial literature which honours the country and the epoch." She attributes the plot of *The Fixed Period* to Trollope's own "sad and serious convictions" about old age and death.

253. Oliphant, Mrs. "Anthony Trollope," *Living Age*, 156 (24 February, 1883), 507-510.

This is a reprint of the article which first appeared in *Good Words* (see above, Entry 242.).

254. Edwards, Amelia B. "Voice from the Tomb," *Literary World*, 14 (14 March, 1883), 94-95.

In a column she writes for this journal as its English correspondent, Ms. Edwards reminisces about her acquaintance with Anthony Trollope, and especially about a conversation she had with him about his life style and work habits. She reports on his habit of writing so much every day, in the morning before breakfast, and his happiness and facility in writing.

255. Unsigned. "Smoking and Drinking," *Pall Mall Gazette*, 37 (15 March, 1883), 1-2.

This is a review of a book by A. A. Reade, entitled *Study and Stimulants*. For the volume, Mr. Reade interviewed prominent people about their smoking and drinking habits and the effect of these habits on their work and their lives in general. Trollope is mentioned as one interviewee who strongly defended smoking.

256. Unsigned. "The Novels of Anthony Trollope," *The Dublin Review*, 92, o.s. (April, 1883), 314-334.

This reviewer opens with a biography of Trollope, and treats chiefly the novels of the Barchester series. He notes that some of the most interesting characters are past middle age, and finds this a virtue. The true object of fiction, he declares, is "to amuse and entertain us in a leisure hour without exciting us to an uneasy pitch or harrowing our sympathies over the sorrows of imaginary beings . . . ." "This end Trollope virtually always achieves." The reviewer feels the characterization of Lily Dale is superb, and that hers is a "perfect love." Certain of the women characters are objected to as tasteless and unrealistic, notably Mabel Grex and Lady Eustace. The reviewer also notes that the predominantly Roman Catholic readers of this journal will find nothing in Trollope offensive to their beliefs, although Trollope seems to think that the highest goal a person can attain is "to marry and live happily ever after," which is somewhat limited.

257. Unsigned. Untitled, *Literary World,* 14 (21 April, 1883), 124.

Review of *Kept in the Dark.* The reviewer praises this latest of Trollope's works in a very brief notice. He comments that the story is "pleasantly related in Mr. Trollope's best vein."

258. Unsigned. "Novels of the Week," *Athenaeum,* 2898 (12 May 1883), 600.

Review of *Mr. Scarborough's Family.* The reviewer comments that this novel is in Trollope's usual entertaining style, then gives a synopsis of the plot and praises the characters as "well-drawn."

259. [Pollack, W. H.]. "Anthony Trollope," *Harper's New Monthly Magazine,* 66 (May 18, 1883), 907-912.

This reviewer notes that Trollope's ease and quickness of writing may mask for some the great skill required in the production of such a large number of novels. Pollack admires Trollope's deep knowledge of human nature and human possibilities, and remarks that the novelist in fact worked on his novels all day, every day; he turned the characters around in his mind until he knew them as well as he knew close friends. Pollack asserts that as a friend of Trollope's, he often spoke with him about his writing, and can thus speak knowledgeably about it. He adds that Trollope disliked taking sides in the fictional disputes he created, preferring to let the characters work them out; only occasionally, as when Johnny Eames gave Adolphus Crosbie a black eye, did the novelist become an advocate. Pollack describes Trollope personally as a high-minded and gifted man, very well read and a pleasure to know. Trollope always wanted, he says, to write a history of fiction, but never began it. Pollack thinks that a good thing, as he considers the biography of Thackeray one of his least satisfactory works. He praises Trollope as being especially friendly and helpful to younger writers, a rare quality; he feels that Trollope's loss will be felt very strongly for a long time by all those who knew him.

260. Unsigned. "Mr. Scarborough's Family," *Saturday Review,* 55 (19 May, 1883), 642-643.

This writer expresses regret at having to say that this novel is a "comparative failure," and also at not being able to look forward to another novel from Trollope. Its faults aside, the reviewer notes, "there is an abundance of 'go' in it; there are many striking scenes; and there is one character [Mr. Scarborough] at least which is original." The chief fault in the novel is repetition; the same material is gone over again and again. Although the story is not truly original, it does have variety, he admits, and concludes with his regret at Trollope's death.

261. James, Henry. "Anthony Trollope," *Century*, 26 (July, 1883), 385-395.

James begins with the commendation that Trollope "had much to tell us about English life," but feels that he sacrificed quality to quantity. He describes Trollope's regular work habits, noting that although "his fecundity was prodigious," "he abused his gift, overworked it, rode his horse too hard," to be truly great. James takes Trollope to task for not taking novel-writing seriously as a form of art, not having a solid theory of the novel from which to work. He claims that Trollope was a master of detail, and thus wrote "pictures" instead of stories. He calls Trollope's habit of reminding readers that his stories are fictions "a pernicious trick," an act of being "deliberately inartistic." James insists that the narrator must be a historian or nothing at all. He considers *The Last Chronicle of Barset* to be Trollope's greatest success, because in it he created "honest pathos." All of Trollope's work is very unified, he feels, and every detail adds to the working out of the plot; although he wrote primarily for his own time, Trollope's works may last into the future, for, James feels, he "helped the heart of man to know itself."

262. Unsigned. "Contemporary Literature: Belles Lettres," *Westminster Review* (120 (July, 1883), 148.

Review of *Mr. Scarborough's Family*. In this single-paragraph review, the writer comments favorably on the plot and characterization as "solid and realistic."

263. Unsigned. "Reviews," *Pall Mall Gazette*, 38 (18 July, 1883), 5.

Review of *Mr. Scarborough's Family*. Unlike many of Trollope's novels which were such pleasant surprises to this reviewer — he mentions specifically *The Duke's Children* — this one is not worthy of its author. The reviewer feels that Trollope's "mechanical ways of writing" tended to produce weaker novels as he grew older. About this one, he feels the "plot is a good one, so far as it goes," but that is not enough to outweigh the "weakness and triviality." This novel, he concludes, only makes one remember the Barchester series more fondly.

264. Unsigned. Untitled Note, London *Times*, 28 September, 1883, p. 3.

This is a brief announcement that the autobiography which Trollope wrote in 1876 is currently being prepared for publication. It will give an account, the writer notes, of the poverty and misery of Trollope's childhood, and a frank record of his literary life and his opinions on fiction writing and the place of fiction in literature.

265. Unsigned. "Trollope and Turgenieff," *Literary World*, 14 (6 October, 1883), 327.

This article is a comparison of two short stories: Turgenieff's "Three Meetings" and Trollope's "La Mere Beuche." The reviewer notes the credibility of Trollope's characters, and the facts told us about them. The Russian author often merely suggests things, and his stories contain many mysteries. The reviewer concludes that the writers are equally compelling and imaginative, although they have quite different approaches to the short story.

266. Unsigned. "Trollope's Autobiography," London *Times*, 12 October, 1883, p. 10.

In this first of a two-part review, the writer notes some similarities between Trollope and Dickens, in that they both turned their unhappy childhoods to some account by writing of them.

He notes that this book is "most interesting and delightful reading," and that in it Trollope is "absolutely unreserved, although nothing unpleasantly personal is here." He remarks on the theme of "manly perseverance" evident in Trollope's life, and offers a summary of the *Autobiography* through the publication of *Dr. Thorne*.

267. Unsigned. "Literature," *Athenaeum*, 2920 (13 October, 1883), 457-459.

Review of the *Autobiography*. This reviewer recounts the life of Trollope, including a number of quotations from the work. He notes that the chapters on literary criticism are the words of an expert. He concludes by commending Trollope as an outstanding human being.

268. —. "Trollope's Autobiography," London *Times*, 13 October, 1883, p. 8.

In the concluding segment of a two-part review, the writer continues the synopsis of Trollope's life. He spends a good bit of attention in this article on Trollope's own critical reviews. He considers that Trollope undervalues *Dr. Thorne* as a novel, and that he is too hard on Lily Dale. In the light of Trollope's remarks about his methods of writing, this reviewer insists that there is indeed inspiration in all good writing, and that Trollope is foolish to think that his discipline alone produced his good work. The reviewer concludes by noting that the characters which are the most outstanding are Plantagenet Palliser, Lady Glencora, and Mr. Crawley.

269. Unsigned. "Reviews," *Pall Mall Gazette*, 38 (October 15, 1883), 11-12.

Review of *An Autobiography*. The reviewer declares that Trollope never wrote anything more vivid or graphic than this account of his life. It is absolutely frank, which will, he feels, make it deservedly popular; he finds it one of the best autobiographies published in years. He proceeds to offer an extended synopsis of the volume, concluding with a list of Trollope's publications and the profits he says they brought.

270. Unsigned. "Anthony Trollope," *Saturday Review,* 56 (20 October, 1883), 505-506.

Review of *An Autobiography.* This reviewer feels that no more genuine nor more interesting biography has been published since Trevelyan's study of his father. He notes Trollope's praise for Ireland and his assertions that his life from that time on was good and pleasant. The reviewer skims trough the major events in Trollope's life and his opinions on fiction. He praises Trollope for having common sense, unlike many other critics and writers. He notes that the novelist does not once mention the many kindnesses he performed for others, and concludes that the work is that of a very fine and admirable man.

271. Morley, John, and Mary Ward. "Anthony Trollope," *Macmillan's* 49 (November, 1883), 47-56.

Review of *An Autobiography.* These two writers present an extended account of Trollope's life, with numerous quotations. They remark that the stress of the work is on the growth of the author's imagination, and is thus superior to, say, George Sand's autobiography. They judge that he succeeded as he wished in having his novels both entertain and teach. They defend his notion that diligence is more important than inspiration in writing.

272. Unsigned. "Autobiography of Anthony Trollope," *Blackwood's Edinburgh Magazine,* 134 (November, 1883), 577-593.

This reviewer seems to have known Trollope personally, and comments warmly on the man as a person and friend. He proceeds to retell at some length the story of Trollope's life, and includes a fair number of passages from the *Autobiography*. Trollope is praised for his honesty, modesty, and abiding sense of humor, all of which the reviewer finds amply illustrated in this work.

273. [Tanzer, A.] "Anthony Trollope," *The Nation,* 37 (8 November, 1883), 396-397.

Review of *Autobiography*. Tanzer praises the hold on the reader's interest which he finds here. He remarks that this volume is free from Trollope's frequent faults of "prolixity and repetition." Mr. Trollope has not a lot to tell here, the reviewer notes, but he does tell it skillfully, with humor much more evident than in the novels. The quality most admirable in this novel is its candor. The reviewer then summarizes the life outlined in the *Autobiography,* and concludes with the notation that Trollope provided "much innocent amusement" to "tends of thousands of readers who were greatly in need of it."

274. Unsigned. "Novels of the Week," *Athenaeum,* 2926 (24 November, 1883), 665-666.

Review of *The Land-Leaguers*. This book is here regarded as more interesting than many of Trollope's novels, as the characters are rather unusual for him. This writer finds the treatment of Irish politics particularly good. He sketches the plot of the novel, notes that it is a "sombre story," and praises the characterization.

275. Hawthorne, Julian. "The Maker of Many Books," *Manhattan: A Publication for Oddfellows,* 2 (December, 1883), 572-578.

The writer begins this article with an account of his meeting with Anthony Trollope, the latter's appearance and manner. He notes how genial the British author was: "I believe that no man in London society is more generally liked than Anthony Trollope." He proceeds to describe him as a genteel, "honest, clean," quick-tempered, but generous man. Hawthorne then summarizes the *Autobiography*. In discussing Trollope's views of writing, the American notes, "how much good soever Mr. Trollope may have done as a preacher and moralist, he has done great harm to English fictitious literature by his novels," and expresses the wish "that his books might have died, and he lived on indefinitely." Hawthorne does not specifically criticize any novel, but seems to find Trollop's fascination with "commonplaceness" and his "vital sympathy" with the mundane to be weaknesses.

276. Unsigned. "Autobiography of Anthony Trollope," *Living Age*, 159 (8 December, 1883), 579-593.

This is a reprint of an article in *Blackwood's Edinburgh Magazine* in November, 1883. (See above, entry 272).

277. Unsigned. Untitled, *Literary World*, 14 (15 December, 1883), 442-443.

Review of *An Autobiography*. The reviewer declares that this book is as good as any of Trollope's novels, which the journal's readers must already know the reviewer likes. He urges everyone who has the modest price of the volume to purchase it immediately. He outlines Trollope's adult life and quotes several passages from the work, including the list of earnings realized from the publications. He finds the same "good human" qualities evident here as are in the novels.

278. Unsigned. Untitled, *Pall Mall Gazette*, 36 (16 December, 1883), 4

In a column with several others items, are excerpts from a letter from "the vicar of the Sussex village" where Trollope used to live. The letter is a tribute to Trollope the man, noting his generosity to the poor, his regular church attendance, and his fervor for the right; he was, the unnamed vicar declares, "the perfect type of gentle English manhood and honour."

279. MacLeod, Donald. "Anthony Trollope," *Good Words,* 25 (1884), 248-252.

Review of *An Autobiography.* Mr. Macleod recounts the story of Trollope's life as revealed in the *Autobiography* and from his personal knowledge of the novelist. He gives the magazines's side of the refusal to publish, in 1863, the novel, *Rachel Ray,* and quotes from the letter that the editor, Macleod's brother, wrote to Trollope about the matter at the time. He declares that the issue was not the "wholesomeness" of the story, which was never in dispute, but rather the presentation of several church people in an unfavorable light; the editor felt that this would be disastrous to the magazine, in the light of its known readership. He remarks that the relationship between the magazine and the author continued long after this incident, and was warm and friendly.

280. [Austin, Alfred, or Meetkerke, Cecilia]. "Last Reminiscences of Anthony Trollope." *Temple Bar,* 70 (January, 1884), 129-134.

Whichever of these friends of Trollope wrote this article uses the occasion of the publication of the *Autobiography* to comment on the years between its completion (1876) and Trollope's death. The writer relates a few anecdotes illustrating Trollope's kindness, humor, and bustling manner which continued until his fatal illness.

281. Shand, Alexander I. "The Literary Life of Anthony Trollope," *Edinburgh Review*, 159 (January, 1884), 186-212.

> Review of the *Autobiography*. Shand discusses Trollope's life, especially his expressed thoughts about a writer's habits of work, responsibilities, and the like. Shand thinks Trollope compares well with Dickens, Scott, and Thackeray, in terms of the balance of diligence and inspiration in his writing. He proceeds to a consideration of the difficulties which younger writers, and especially women, face in choosing to pursue a literary career, in light of the current decline in the sale (and presumably the reading) of novels. Shand concludes by placing Trollope in a line (with Dickens and Thackeray) descending directly from Richardson.

282. Whitehurst, E. C. "Anthony Trollope," *Westminster Review*, 121 (January, 1884), 83-115.

> Review of *An Autobiography*. Whitehurst defines the object of reading this work: "to see what lessons we can learn from his life and character." He suggests that there are many worthwhile lessons here, and offers a synopsis of the work with numerous quotations.

283. Johnson, Edward. "The Rewards of Authorship," *Literary World*, 15 (12 January, 1884), 9.

> This is a letter to the magazine's editor, on the subject of the money earned by various authors. He mentions Trollope's account of his earnings which appeared in the *Autobiography*; he also estimates Frances Trollope's literary earnings, and those of a number of 18th and 19th century writers.

284. Unsigned. "Some Novels," *Saturday Review*, 57 (12 January, 1884), 53-54.

Review of *The Land Leaguers.* If finished, the reviewer says, this novel would have done Trollope no discredit; in it he shows the knowledge of Ireland that was seen in his very earliest works, plus the advantage of his intervening years of experience in writing. The ideas in it, he says, would have been startling had they appeared when *Barchester Towers* was written, but they are no longer so. The reviewer summarizes the plot and notes that Trollope here makes a very strong case against British policies in Ireland.

285. Unsigned. "Mr. Trollope's Last Novel," *Saturday Review,* 57 (29 March, 1884), 414-415.

Review of *An Old Man's Love.* The writer notes that this novel is more finished than *The Land Leaguers,* and is "not an unfitting finale to an almost unparalleled series of works in fiction." He outlines the plot and says it contains one of the best pieces of soul-dissection that Trollope ever did, in the character of Mr. Whittlestaff. He mentions several other characters and describes them briefly, and concludes with strong praise of the narration.

286. Unsigned. "Novels of the Week," *Athenaeum,* 2945 (5 April, 1884), 438.

Review of *An Old Man's Love.* This is a brief, very positive review. It presents an account of the plot and high praise for the characterization of Mr. Whittlestaff.

287. Unsigned. "An Old Man's Love," London *Times,* 14 April, 1884, p. 3.

This reviewer notes that Trollope usually needed more "elbow room" in a story than a one-volume publication allowed; but this novel he finds is "unusually compact and complete." He also finds here evidence of "a striking command both of humour and pathos." He offers a plot summary, emphasizing the characterization, and concludes that this work "leaves us with agreeable memories of its lamented writer almost at his very best."

288. Unsigned. Untitled, *Literary World*, 15 (3 May, 1884), 147.

Review of *An Old Man's Love*. The novel is described as "pleasant" by this reviewer, though it is classed as among his lesser works. The plot is outlined, and the reviewer notes there are "amusing people" in it.

289. Payn, James. "Some Literary Recollections: VIII," *Cornhill Magazine*, 3, n.s. (July, 1884), 41-58.

In commenting on a number of novelists including Dickens, Thackeray, Charles Reade, and others, he notes of Trollope that he was "the least literary man of letters I ever met," although he was "the last of the great triumvirate of modern novelists." Payn asserts that the creation of memorable characters is the truest test of great novelists; many contemporary novels contain none at all. However, Dickens, Thackeray, and Trollope certainly do. He asserts regretfully that Trollope injured his own reputation by talking about his methods of writing, and that Trollope never properly admired Thackeray because the latter was not methodical enough.

290. Wedgewood, Julia. "Contemporary Records II — Fiction," *Contemporary Review*, 46 (July, 1884), 149-151.

Review of *An Old Man's Love*. This reviewer has few kind words for the final novel. She declares that one would not pay much attention to this "languid and colourless little sketch," if it were not known to be the final work of Anthony Trollope. It does, however, remind one of his other works, she notes. She compares Trollope to Thackeray, noting that Trollope is to Thackeray as Thackeray is to Fielding. Trollope wrote for women primarily, she says, while Thackeray wrote for both men and women. While Trollope's view of life may not be "elevating," she finds it is "pure and "healthful," and his influence is always toward what is "gentle and true." While Thackeray makes the reader feel scorn for his characters, she remarks, Trollope makes one feel compassion. She then summarizes the plot of *An Old Man's Love*, remarking particularly the character of the house-keeper and what she feels is Trollope's over-generous treatment of Mr. Whittlestaff.

291. Unsigned. "About Novels," *Literary World*, 15 (23 August, 1884), 275.

This article consists of a series of quotations from other periodicals on the topic in question. There is quoted a passage from *Contemporary Review* (see above, entry 290) to the effect that Thackeray wrote for men readers, and Trollope for women, with the result that Thackeray will be read longer than will Trollope.

292. Unsigned. "English Character and Manners as Portrayed by Anthony Trollope," *Westminster Review*, 123 (January, 1885), 53-100.

This writer discusses various facets of "English character" as he finds them treated in Trollope's fiction. He feels Trollope presents the British very truly. Among the topics he considers are foxhunting, patterns of conversation (including ways of evading a question, polite methods of argument, typical expressions of affection), relationships between parents and children, and businessmen's behavior.

293. Unsigned. Untitled, *Pall Mall Gazette*, 41 (14 January, 1885), 3.

This writer announces that he will summarize an extended critique of Trollope in the *Temps*. He notes that the article in question is rather disparaging to Trollope, but does conclude on a positive note: as a person — husband, father, employee of the post office — Trollope has done a very good job; if he is not truly memorable as a novelist, yet he is superior to many others.

294. Unsigned. Untitled, *Literary World,* 16 (21 February, 1885), 67.

This brief note calls attention to the fact that an article about Anthony Trollope appeared in the January issue of *Westminster Review*. (See above, entry 292).

295. Unsigned. "Reviews," *Pall Mall Gazette,* 51 (11 November, 1887), 3.

Review of Thomas A. Trollope's *What I Remember*. This review of Anthony Trollope's brother's autobiography begins by mentioning Anthony's works. The reviewer also particularly highlights the part Anthony played in his brother's book — recounting a dispute with Elizabeth Barrett Browning over whether an artist must give up his or her "ordinary humanity" in order to succeed, and also the introduction of Anthony to the Carlyles.

296. Unsigned. "Literary Notes and Echoes," *Pall Mall Gazette,* 51 (12 November, 1887), 6.

The writer of this article cites the Trollope family as prolific "paper-stainers." He estimates, he says conservatively, that Mrs. Trollope published 115 books, Anthony 100, Thomas Adolphus 50, and Theodosia (Mrs. T. A.) 10. He mentions the dispute between Anthony Trollope and Mrs. Browning which Thomas recounts in his autobiography, and he compliments Anthony for an emendation he suggested for a line of one of Mrs. Browning's poems.

297. Unsigned. Untitled, *Pall Mall Gazette,* 49 (3 August, 1889), 3.

This is a review article about a book, *Memorable London Houses,* by Wilmot Harrison. The book is particularly recommended for those readers with "a literary turn of mind," as among the houses described and illustrated in the volume are those of Anthony Trollope, George Eliot, Charles Dickens, and other writers. The review notes that the book claims that Anthony Trollope died ultimately from the irritant effects of barrel organs in the house at 39 Montague Square.

298. Unsigned. "Fiction as Favorite," *Pall Mall Gazette,* 40 (3 September, 1889), 7.

This article, written in response to an article by Mr. Gattie in the *Fortnightly Review* (date not cited), on the popularity of certain fiction, mentions that the works of Anthony Trollope, as well as those of Mrs. Gaskell, "seem to be completely out of fashion," based on a survey of lending library records. The survey is reported to prove that "novels about today" are much in demand.

299. Unsigned. "Mr. Trollope's Autobiography Again," *Pall Mall Gazette,* 49 (2 November, 1889), 3.

This is a review of Volume 3 of Thomas A. Trollope's autobiography. The reviewer begins by commenting on the volubility of all the "Trollope tribe." He then quotes from this autobiography some remarks about Thomas' and Anthony's friendly comparison of the amounts of their published work; the comparison revealed that Anthony had more books, and Thomas more "writing" of various kinds published. The revierwer speculates doubtfully about the lasting qualities of both men's works, and remarks that at least they both were able to earn enough by writing to live one, which is more of an accomplishment than many people realize.

300. Harrison, Frederic. "Anthony Trollope's Place in Literature," *Forum,* 19 (May, 1895), 324-337.

Mr. Harrison begins by saying that young readers of the 90s do not value Anthony Trollope's work; but he, who knew Trollope well, claims for him a definite place in history, despite Trollope's "modest claims and conspicuous faults, of his prolixity, his limited sphere, his commonplaces." Harrison praises the geniality and modest egoism revealed in *An Autobiography.* He notes the industry of Trollope's work habits, and remarks that his worst writing is no poorer than that of Bulwer, Disraeli, and even Dickens. He claims that Trollope always writes "pure, bright, graceful English" about "wholesome men and women," and that on occasion, Trollope has written "with a really exquisite grace and consummate truth." Trollope's style he admires though it is not equal to Thackeray's, since he admires his naturalness in speech, which Harrison attributes to the speed of composition. The dialogues he describes as "stenographic" in their realism, and much superior to those of Richardson, Fielding, Goldsmith, or Scott. Trollope produced, of his 60 books, ten that are worth re-reading, among them the Barchester series. He attributes Trollope's current bad reputation as due to the age's demand for the exotic and the sensational, and predicts that Trollope's reputation, especially for his best works, will revive and last. He concludes by saying that four-fifths of Trollope's work should be burned, but that the rest will last long into the future.

301. Gwynn, Stephen. "Anthony Trollope," *Macmillan's,* 81 (January, 1900), 217-226.

Gwynn here offers a review of Trollope's novels generally, noting that they are no longer so widely read as previously. He regrets this, and praises the characterization in particular. Gwynn finds that Trollope's well-known diligence in writing, however, often worked against true excellence; he feels that Trollope often padded "outrageously." Trollope writes in the same vein as Jane Austen, he says, although she surpassed him at creating "masterpieces out of trivialities." He feels that Trollope's "wide acquaintance with life" gave meat to his work, and insists that Trollope's characters and actions are better because truer to life, than those in any of the best selling fiction of 1900.

302. Peck, Horace Thurston. "Anthony Trollope," *Bookman*, 13 (April,, 1901), 114-125.

This is a reprint of the Introduction to the Royal Edition of Trollope's novels published by the Gebbie Company of Philadelphia in 1900. The writer declares that Anthony Trollope is the "most typically English" of all writers of English fiction. He cites Hawthorne's early praise, recounts Trollope's life and presents a list of his published works. He thinks the revelations about his regular writing in the *Autobiography* have hurt Trollope's reputation; he thinks too that the French naturalism movement, as evidenced in Zola's works, have hurt Trollope. Naturalistic works, often brutal and gross, possess a morbid fascination for new readers — "the cult of the unmentionable." Peck thinks, however, that this trend, which he likens to an infection, seems to have nearly run its course, and healthier tastes will return. He sees Trollope as standing close to the best of the "true realists," and as better at a wider scope of life than Thackeray, although he is less deep.

Articles By Trollpe

T1. [Trollope, Anthony]. "My Tour in Holland," *The Cornhill Magazine,* 6 (November, 1862), 616-622.

This personal, friendly essay addresses the reader directly as "you" quite frequently. Trollope remarks that most English people have an incorrect picture of the Dutch people's size, appearance, and habits. (They are small, neat, and generally merry but virtually never intoxicated.) He relates some humorous anecdotes about his experiences with bathing machines (superior to those in U.K.) and language difficulties. His trip was made primarily to visit several art museums. He found some "masterpieces" not so impressive as he had anticipated; the lighting in Dutch museums is not good. He mentions several museums, and several specific paintings which he saw, and his admittedly non-academic opinions of them. He describes town life, hotel service, village fairs, and the like, and remarks that he thoroughly enjoyed his trip to Holland.

T2. Trollope, Anthony. "W. M. Thackeray," *The Cornhill Magazine,* 9 (February, 1864), 134-137.

This is essentially a personal tribute to Thackeray as a friend, and as the editor of *Cornhill* who resigned because he found it unpleasant to say "no" to so many. Trollope hopes biographers will be fair to the man; he considers *Esmond* the finest of Thackeray's works, as it has "a completeness of historical plot, and an absence of that taint of unnatural life which blemishes, perhaps, all other historical novels." Trollope views Colonel Newcome as "the finest single character in English fiction," surpassed only in all fiction by Don Quixote. He closes with the assertion that there should be a bust of Thackeray installed in Westminster Abbey.

T3. Trollope, Anthony. "England and America," *Pall Mall Gazette*, 1 (February 26, 1865), 3.

In this letter to the editor, Trollope insists that this journal's editorial advice for readers to remain neutral on the American Civil War is wrong-headed. The British government must remain neutral, he explains, but the people individually should not. They should make an effort to be informed, which many do not. He defends the North's position on unity and abolition, and remarks that we may admire the gallantry of the southerners but should not let that admiration obscure the truth that the South will lose, and should lose, and that slavery in North America will finally be ended.

T4. —. "The American Conflict," *Pall Mall Gazette*, 1 (March 30, 1865), 162-163.

In this extended letter to the editor, Trollope asserts that the real reason for the American Civil War is the question of slavery. He discusses the feelings of various segments of the United States about slavery, and predicts that the Union will survive and be better for this conflict. American people will learn, he says, that they must atone for the evil they have done and this will humble them before the other nations of the world.

T5. —. "Henry Taylor's Poems," *Fortnightly Review*, 1 (29 May, 1865), 129-146.

Here Trollope speaks favorably of the current trend toward praising a poet while he still lives instead of waiting a century; he notes that Tennyson and Browning are able to enjoy the critics' plaudits. Henry Taylor is another living poet who has already achieved fame — in fact his earlier published works were more highly regarded than his more recent works. This volume collects all the poems; Trollope discusses several of them specifically, remarking that an early piece, "Van Artveld," still seems to him the best and most lasting of the collection. He characterizes it as thoughtful but not difficult to follow; he criticizes a few phrases as "terribly inflated;" among these are "the gibbous moon" and "the vegetable dead." Taylor's works deserve more recognition than they have thus far been given, Trollope concludes.

T6. —. "On Anonymous Literature," *Fortnightly Review*, 1 (1 July, 1865), 491-498.

Trollope argues for the signing of all periodical articles, as is the custom in France. Authors should be responsible for their work. There is some justification, he feels, for newspapers to print unsigned political articles; but for non-political writing, there is no valid argument for anonymity. Critics would be fewer but better, Trollope is certain, if they had to sign their criticism. He feels that often critics do not even read the books they review (the blame for this lies partly with the low rate of pay for reviewers). Signatures would force an honesty and a "real criticism" which is seen now only too rarely.

T7. —. "Notices of New Books," *Fortnightly Review*, 1 (15 July, 1865), 633-635.

Review of *Sesame and Lilies*, by John Ruskin. Trollope notes that Mr. Ruskin is a wonderful and powerful art critic, as seen in his earlier writings. This work fails, however, as Ruskin is not a good political economist or preacher, Trollope asserts.

He finds Ruskin's 'poetic expression' still evident here, but notes a lack of "innate conspicuous wisdom." He wryly summarizes the advice in *Sesame and Lilies,* inserting many exclamation marks, and advises Ruskin to return to art history and criticism, his true metier.

T8. —. "The Irish Church," *Fortnightly Review,* 2 (15 August, 1865), 82-90.

Trollope discusses the coming inevitable demise of the Irish Church Establishment, and responds to two recent pamphlets concerning this issue. He notes agreement with Alfred Lee's position that the establishment is indefensible, but takes issue with Lee's proposal to give the funds to the Protestant Church of Ireland. He argues also against Maziere Brady's proposed formula for dividing the funds among various church groups; Trollope insists that the final formula must include all the citizens of Ireland, and the Roman Catholics must get their proportional share of the revenues.

T9 —. "Notices of New Books," *Fortnightly Review,* 2 (1 September, 1865), 255-256.

Review of *Characters and Criticisms,* by James Hannay. Trollope notes that this is a collection of essays from a wide range of periodicals. He cites individual articles and summarizes the contents. He praises these articles as accurate and honest, not flawed as Hannay's articles sometimes are by the writer's political biases. The writing Trollope characterizes as "graphic English, terse and yet flowing." The only flaw he finds is the occasionally obvious malice toward a person or issue.

T10. —. "Notices of New Books," *Fortnightly Review,* 2 (15 September, 1865), 379-380.

Review of *The Day and The Hour,* by Capt. W. A. Baker.

Trollope sketches a summary of this work, which is a set of prophecies based on Baker's reading of the Bible, and declares it absolutely incredible. He suggests that Baker, a man of some reputation as a mathematician, will be thought insane as a result of this work.

T11. —. "Public Schools," *Fortnightly Review,* 2 (1 October, 1865), 476-487.

This article is a call for school reform. Tradition, Trollope feels, is over-reverenced in England, even when traditions create obviously negative effects. Today, he says, the schools need more teachers, better management of the moneys, more innovation in teaching methods, and less restrictive admission requirements (the "native of England" rule is truly pointless). Furthermore, Trollope insists, the plans for reform should be made in consultation with the people directly involved and familiar with the present school system.

T12. —. "The Civil Service," *Fortnightly Review,* 2 (15 October, 1865), 613-626.

This article was written in response to a report of the Civil Service Commissioners. Trollope objects to the fact that the commissioners are not answerable to the public for their actions. He has no complaints about their actions, but a system should be devised to allow for the registration and action upon complaints should they arise. He discusses the values and the dangers involved in both patrongage and examination-based appointments. He remarks on the unreasonable demands and scarcity of rewards of much civil service work, and notes that this will prevent capable young people from entering the field, and should be changed.

T13. —. "Clergymen of the Church of England," *Pall Mall Gazette,* 2 (November 20, 1865), 1093-1094.

Part 1 (of ten parts): The Modern English Archbishop. Trollope begins by describing the customs and rules pertaining to the office of Archbishops: historically, they must be noblemen, peers in the Parliament. They are, thus, very hard for the average person to approach, and quite mysterious as to their duties. Although they are no longer minor princes, he asserts, they have retained the royal life style. The Prime Minister now appoints them, and they have less income and less power than in former days, but not too much less. Once named, an archbishop holds the title for life, even if proved insane. No one can take the title from him. The Prime Minister's responsibility is thus very grave; he must pick someone, says Trollope, who will seem to be controlling things, but who will not actually do so. The P.M. must find one "great enough to fill it and yet small enough" not to exert his theoretical powers. The appointing of Bishops poses the same problem, but on a less grand scale. Trollope declares that "In the religion of today, moderation is everything;" thus the P.M is always looking for moderates for the posts of Archbishop. The ideal contemporary Archibishop, Trollope says, should answer his correspondence, but with words that mean as little as possible; he should have "diligence, considerable skill, imperturbable good-humour, and undying patience" to deal with the complexities of his office. Judged on these principles, the choices made during the past twenty-five years or so have been very good.

T14. —. "Clergymen of the Church of England," *Pall Mall Gazette*, 2 (November 27, 1865), 1169-1170.

Part 2: English Bishops Old and New. The most obvious difference between modern bishops and their predecessors is the contemporary lack of wigs and the smaller apron. Bishops used to be wealthy barons who lived like lords; then the Church was not known for the piety or theological knowledge of its bishops — in fact, Trollope says, it is amazing that the Church survived the old Bishops. Lately, though, due in large part to the Oxford Movement, bishops must work at their jobs, and surely must earn the 5000£ or so per year. The Bishop still traditionally gives the best livings in his jurisdiction to his friends; and marriage to his daughter is "one of the fairest steps to promotion." Trollope notes sarcastically that this is the last of the professions to practice favoritism openly; even the civil service has been cleaned of sinecures and patronage, and it is "curious" that the Church has not been so revised.

T15. —. "Clergymen of the Church of England," *Pall Mall Gazette*, 2 (December 2, 1865), 1233-1234.

Part 3: The Normal Dean of the Present Day. "When cathedral services were kept up for the honour of God rather than for the welfare of the worshippers, with an understanding . . . that recompense would be given by the Almighty for the honour done to Him . . ," it was natural that one person have the task of overseeing all the workings of the cathedral, and even of adding "tone" to the church, according to Trollope. Nowadays, he reports, the Dean seems to be in charge solely of the building and its impressive appearance to visitors. Trollope adds that modern deans receive "only a thousand pounds" per year, but they have pleasanter and less demanding work than Bishops, who earn much more. Deans are now former active parsons who usually have a taste for literature; they are good students, not driven by a sense of vocation. Trollope adds that deans keep the cathedral and adjunct buildings attractive with help from various ladies' fund-raising groups. The Prime Minister now permits the Chapter to meet and appoint the Dean of the cathedral, and, exclaims Trollope in conclusion, "How English it all is! How picturesque!"

T16. —. "Clergymen of the Church of England," *Pall Mall Gazette*, 2 (December 11, 1865), 1333-1334.

132 Articles By Trollope

Part 4: The Archdeacon. This person, Trollope says, has a good deal more to do than the Dean, and receives a good deal less for doing it. As he receives no stipend or a very small one, the Bishop regularly appoints him to a living (often a very good one). Archdeacons, the writer observes, are often related by blood or marriage to the Bishop. They are expected to be men of the world, and to be very well-informed about the lives of their rectors and vicars. They must be, Trollope adds, alert to any news or suspicion of scandal or private peccadilloes of their underling clergy. Archdeacons should not be personally ambitious, he adds, for once appointed, they will probably hold the post for life. Ideally, they should be gentlemen — i.e., jovial and still superior.

T17. —. "Clergymen of the Church of England," *Pall Mall Gazette*, 2 (December 18, 1865), 1417-1418.

Part 5: The Parson of the Parish. Trollope opens with some remarks on the title "parson," and the variants of "rector" and "vicar." He finds the parson the most attractive form of English clergy, and remarks that the higher a man rises in the church above this post, the less he will be a true clergyman. General feeling dictates that a parson be a gentleman, Trollope notes, so he will be the unquestioned equal of the local squire. Usually a parson's education is at Oxford or Cambridge, and even rustics can detect his social class. While on the whole a humane and kindly man, parsons generally are quite definite in their belief that everyone should belong to the Church of England. Trollope describes them as earnest but not zealous, able to live in a comfortable but not magnificent home, and deserving their reputation as good, honest, comfortable men.

T18. —. "Clergymen of the Church of England," *Pall Mall Gazette*, 2 (December, 1865), 1538.

Part 6: The Town Incumbent. Trollope begins by noting that

no clerical aspirant would choose to be an incumbent if he could be a parson proper. An incumbent has a town district, with a church from which he "draws what income he may make." His status, Trollope asserts, is lower than that of his country colleagues; he must rent a house in town and thus hardly knows the people he preaches to. His income depends solely on how many people attend his services. He can prosper by being an outstanding public speaker; he will never prosper by visiting the poor. His position encourages him to win fame as a speaker, rather than to do other, helpful things. Trollope notes that most incumbents finally do not prosper, but settle back and trudge through their lives on a bare subsistence. This must be remedied, he adds, or the sons of gentlemen will no longer enter the church in adequate numbers; the church has not found a way adequately to deal with growing cities.

T19. —. "Clergymen of the Church of England," *Pall Mall Gazette*, 3 (January 5, 1866), 55-56.

Part 7: The College Fellow Who Has Taken Orders. Trollope here argues that ordination is not always prepared for nor undertaken properly. It is legally the privilege of a Fellow at Oxford or at Cambridge to demand orders; but this right is now questionable, he thinks. The understood duty of a Protestant clergyman is to help others to worship; yet many are ordained who do not have this end in view. Fellows must be celibate; thus, few men want to be Fellows forever. Traditionally, Fellows asked for ordination when they either had the prospect of a living as a clergyman, or wanted to marry, or both. In olden times, Fellows were monks, and intended to be celibate for life; it made sense then to ordain them without other considerations. However, Trollope observes, times and church rules have changed, and customs should change too. Clergymen who have been Fellows in a college until the age of, say, 40, are not the best candidates to take on parish life. We would not even consider licensing other professionals, such as physicians or lawyers, without some sort of apprenticeship; yet, Trollope says, we seem to assume that clergy need no practise in the arena in which they propose to work for the rest of their lives. Ordination should be the conclusion to a course of spiritual preparation, not a routine ceremony performed for temporal or traditional reasons. Fellows should not, therefore, be automatically ordained, nor even automatically considered for ordination. The situation as it now is, encourages all Fellows to demand ordination as a matter of course, instead of encouraging them to think of it as a serious and binding obligation on their parts.

T20. —. "Critical Notices," *Fortnightly Review*, 3 (15 January, 1866), 650-652.

Review of *The Ideas of the Day on Policy*, by Charles Buxton, M.A., M.P. Describing this book as one which purposes "to define what the public opinion in England is on all matters of state politics," Trollope judges this an oddly-intentioned effort. While of little interest to the general reading public, he asserts, it would be useful for men in government to consult. Often these leaders have little idea of what the public feels on a certain issue. Rather atypically here, Trollope mentions neither methodology nor style.

T21. —. "The Fourth Commandment," *Fortnightly Review*, 3 (15 January, 1866), 529-538.

This is a discussion of a sermon to the Presbytery of Glasgow by Dr. Norman Macleod, the editor of *Good Works* magazine, and a minister of the Church of Scotland. In the sermon under discussion, Macleod said that he did not believe in the continual obligation of the 4th commandment [keep holy the sabbath-day]. Trollope supports this view, sketches the history of the observance of the commandment, and notes that it enjoined the Old Testament Jews from labor, but does not require us to spend the entire day in church or in tedious non-activity.

T22. —. "Clergymen of the Church of England," *Pall Mall Gazette*, 3 (January 20, 1866), 217-218.

Part 8: The Curate in a Populous Parish. Trollope insists in this article that of all the clergymen, curates are the most shamelessly exploited, both by the Bishops and by the other clergy. The proportion of work done by these men is the greatest in proportion to the money received by them; this situation is "horrible to the imagination." He considers that the situation is improving slowly — clerical stipends are becoming more equitable (and Bishops' houses are suffering because of this), but any sort of fairness has not reached most curates yet. Trollope feels that no curate can hope to rise on his own merit, nor can he enjoy the social standing, invitations to interesting events, etc., which in former times helped to compensate for the low income. The present arrangement, says Trollope, encourages curates to become soured; this is everywhere apparent, and makes young men chary of entering the church; if this situation is not remedied, the church will be much the poorer for it.

T23. —. "Clergymen of the Church of England," *Pall Mall Gazette*, 3 (January 23, 1866), 244-245.

Part 9: The Irish Beneficed Clergyman. The normal Irish Protestant clergyman is, Trollope observes, a "severe sombre man," preaching in his every motion. This is so because he is surrounded by Roman Catholics, with whom he has no sympathy. His activity is often felt as futile, and he too often sees his work as fighting against enemies, not as helping friends. Irish livings, Trollope notes, are not good; in addition, the men are often isolated. Too often the public believes they are grossly overpaid, because of the relatively few Protestant parishioners in Ireland. Trollope concludes with a call for reform.

T24. —. "Clergymen of the Church of England," *Pall Mall Gazette*, 3 (January 25, 1866), 273-274.

Part 10: The Clergyman Who subscribes for Colenso. In this last article of his series, Trollope discusses and describes the Broad Church clergy, sometimes called "free-thinkers." This movement, he notes, is mostly an urban phenomenon, and is scorned in rural areas, which are more fundamentalist. He criticizes the movement's followers and promoters, as he feels they cause undue speculation and fear among the public. He asserts that they often seem glib and clever in their refutations of such traditions as the seven days of creation, but are very indefinite in describing what exactly they do believe. A sure sign that a clergyman is a free-thinker, Trollope notes, is his giving money to support Colenso; and any traditional believer will consider such a person to be an infidel at best.

T25. —. "Critical Notices," *Fortnightly Review*, 3 (1 February, 1866), 775-777.

Review of *The Red Shirt*, by Albert Mario. Trollope summarizes the plot (an account of Mario's career with Garibaldi), and notes that, although purportedly factual, the narrative seems quite improbable. As history, he judges it a "bad book;" as an expression of admiration for Garibaldi, a good one.

T26. —. "Mr. Anthony Trollope and the *Saturday Review*," *Pall Mall Gazette*, 3 (February 5, 1866), 395.

This item is a letter from Trollope expressing annoyance that he has been scolded publicly for writing to newspapers on matters of public concern. He mentions the *Fortnightly Review* called him to task for writing about the observance of the fourth commandment, and the *Pall Mall Gazette* for writing about Abraham Lincoln. Both papers suggested that he had taken advantage of his fame as a novelist to win attention to his views on matters on which he was by no means expert to speak. He asks in this letter whether the editors of the *Pall Mall Gazette* have no other interests than their jobs, and insists that all citizens should think and write and talk about public issues, and no particular occupation should prevent anyone from doing so. He concludes with a reiteration of his argument in the *Fortnightly Review* about the observance of Sundays.

T27. —. "Critical Notices," *Fortnightly Review*, 5 (15 May, 1866), 126-128.

Review of *Resources and Prosperity of America*, by Sir M. Peto, Bart., M.P. Opening with the back-handed compliment that this is a very dull but useful volume, Trollope describes it as a book of numbers and not of imagination. Trollope summarizes Peto's discussion of American resources, noting his own disagreements on some points, and chides the author for omitting any mention of U. S. public education, which Trollope sees as one of America's greatnesses.

T28. —. "Critical Notices," *Fortnightly Review*, 5 (1 June, 1866), 251-254.

Review of *The Civil War in America: An Address at the Last Meeting of the Manchester Union and Emancipation Society*, by Goldwyn Smith. Trollope contrasts this volume with Morton Peto's book on America (Cf. T27), reviewed in the previous issue of *Fortnightly*, citing the work as "a pamphlet of opinion, not of facts." Trollope points out the features which mark this work as a speech, rather than a written work: "the language is more rhetorical and the reasoning less close." He summarizes the work, noting some points of personal disagreement as to the probable future of the United States. Trollope agrees with Smith in praising the humane attitude of the North toward the South after the Civil War.

T29. —. "Critical Notices," *Fortnightly Review,* 5 (15 June, 1866), 381-384.

Review of *The Crown of Wild Olive. Three Lectures on Work, Traffic, and War,* by John Ruskin. Trollope notes that the language, though "always beautiful," is here "fantastic," and sometimes difficult to follow. He praises Ruskin generally for his perception of beauty and his ability to educate his audience to see line and form in life as well as art. This work, however, is strongly criticized as tedious and containing a great number of unreasonable statements. While Ruskin logically leads toward a denunciation of private property, he does not denounce it. "Mr. Ruskin's fault is, that he has seemed himself to have discovered truth; but that in doing so he has neither used reason, nor, as yet, that 'intense gaze'" [of, say, Carlyle].

T30. —. "Critical Notices," *Fortnightly Review,* 6 (15 October, 1866), 632-636.

Review of *The Life and Death of Jeanne D'Arc,* by Harriet Parr. Trollope praises this book as having the two important virtues of "this kind of book:" it is informative and it is pleasant to read. His humor is evident in his summary of the narrative, as "Her voices . . . told her to go . . . to King Charles VII, who in those days sadly wanted somebody to go to him." Trollope praises the biography as thorough, although perhaps too partisan.

T31. —. "Critical Notices," *Fortnightly Review,* 7 (February, 1867), 252-255.

Review of *The Rose of Cheriton,* by Mrs. Sewell. Trollope points out that this is an essay in verse written avowedly "to lessen the terrible sin of drunkenness to which the working classes are subject" and to encourage Parliament to stop this evil by closing all beer-shops. There is a tone of tired patience in Trollope's comments on this work; after agreeing that drunkenness is very bad, he describes this work as a typical example of "millions" of do-good pamphlets being published. He points out that good intentions do not excuse the publication of illogical, implausible, or inartistic works such as he finds this to be.

T32. —. "Introduction," *Saint Paul's* 1 (October, 1867), 1-7.

As the editor of a newly-founded magazine, Trollope here defends the genre and outlines the policies of *Saint Paul's*. Against the frequent charges that the great number of magazines of the day are essentially trivial, Trollope points out that magazines supplement, rather than replace, "great literature." Furthermore, many great writers reach the public through periodicals on a scale they could not otherwise achieve. *Saint Paul's* will combine entertainment, instruction, politics, and poetry; it will not be a magazine of criticism. It will be open to the well-known and the amateur author alike.

T33. —. "On Sovereignty," *Saint Paul's,* 1 (October, 1867), 76-91.

This is a defense of the constitutional monarchy, such as exists in England, over the "autocratic sovereignty" which is the government of France, and the "elected sovereignty" such as the United States has; Britain's system answers best to the will of the people and the changing political needs of the times, Trollope asserts.

T34. —. "About Hunting," *Saint Paul's,* 1 (November, 1867), 206-219.

Trollope here offers a discussion of fox-hunting as the most thoroughly English recreation, and a defense of it as conducive to good will between social classes. He comments on the effects of railroads on hunting (despite some problems, it has made the sport more accessible to city dwellers). He sketches the changes in hunting in the past century, and discusses the financial problems of Masters of hunts in maintaining a pack and staging hunts. He argues that all who participate should support the sport adequately by subscribing to a particular hunt, and paying the master fairly.

T35. —. "The Uncontrolled Ruffianism of London as Measured by the Rule of Thumb," *Saint Paul's,* 1 (January, 1868), 419-424.

Trollope here offers a humorous denial of the widely-accedpted belief that London is a center of rowdyism and that it is dangerour in the extreme to be out alone, especially after dark. He credits his own experiences and those of his friends (who have never been attacked) as of more importance than the headlines, statistics, and general rumors about the numbers of criminals lying in wait, and he discounts the advice to carry weapons as being more dangerous than the threats they supposedly would protect against.

T36. —. "Whom Shall We Make Leader of the House of Commons?" *Saint Paul's,* 1 (February, 1868), 531-545.

Trollope asserts here that the Leader of the House of Commons is a more important position than is the Prime Minister, and people should be more concerned to plan ahead for the former. Disraeli is now the leader, and may continue for some time; but the liberal party should make up its collective mind as to who their candidate will be, and be ready to act on the instant that it becomes necessary. He notes the practical necessity for members to belong to and work with a political party, even if it means occasionally having to surrender one of one's favorite "crochets" in the interest of unity. The conservatives under Disraeli are evidence of the power of such unity; the liberals should learn from their example. He argues against the notion that it is the issues, not the men, who are important; it is the men who make the issues, he insists, and only by having a majority can good laws be passed with some regularity. He argues that the liberals should rally behind Gladstone, his choice; he mentions several other possibilities, noting their strong and weak points.

T37. —. "About Hunting II," *Saint Paul's*, 1 (March, 1868), 675-690.

Trollope opens by noting that in Part I (Cf T34) he discussed the "nationality" and the costs of hunting. Now he will describe the pleasures of the sport, and the methods of ensuring the pleasures. He notes that there is no real "score" in this sport, as there is in others, to measure one's success by or to take pride in. Despite some rumors to the contrary, it is not a "fast" pastime — wild living and over-drinking are not properly a part of the sport. There is nothing proper to the sport which would be inappropriate for a clergyman to do; in fact, Trollope recommends the sport for clergymen as a wholesome recreation. He discusses the ideal kinds of terrain, weather, and the like, as well as the care required for horses and the authority of the Master of the hunt. He mentions also the courtesy due to those (especially non-hunters) whose property is ridden over during the course of a hunt.

T38. —. "The Irish Church Debate," *Saint Paul's*, 2 (May, 1868), 147-160.

As Trollope sees the issue, there are two points to be considered. The first is the status of the Irish Church; the second is the leadership of the House of Commons — and the second seems to be at the heart of most of the current controversy. Disraeli, now in the minority, is the Prime Minister. The end of English control of the Irish Church is clearly imminent —

the current debate is only nominally about that. He argues against what he perceives as Disraeli's "stalling" techniques. He foresees that there will be a general election within a year's time, after the new Reform Bill begins to operate, and then no doubt a new government will be formed; probably there will be a new prime minster. Mr. Gladstone's recent speech outlining his plans for the disestablishment may have been somewhat premature, in that more planning needs to be done to ensure fairness — but everyone of sense must see that it is now the means and not the fact, of disestablishment, which must be worked out.

T39. —. "American Reconstruction," *Saint Paul's* (September, 1868), 662-675.

Trollope feels strongly that understanding of this matter is essential to understanding the "present political condition of the United States," which is certainly of interest to all reasonably-informed English people. Trollope feels that the central question now is this: "Can a community of white men be made to live in subjugation to a community of negroes, the numbers being, let us say, equal?" Trollope thinks this is not possible, but that it will be the logical outcome of the present system of taxation and other laws established at the end of the Civil War. He gives a rather detailed argument of his understanding of the facts of life in southern parts of the United States; he objects to the theory that blacks are equal to whites as "fatuous," although he feels slavery is a serious moral evil. He argues that political corruption on an enormous scale is one of the inevitable results of the enforcement of Reconstruction laws.

T40. —. "Clarissa," *Saint Paul's,* 3 (November, 1868), 163-172.

Review of an abridged edition of Richardson's novel, by E. S. Dallas. Trollope offers hard criticism of *Clarissa* as a novel, on the grounds that it is prolix, unbelievable, and filled with rogues and even worse characters. It simply is not worth Mr. Dallas' time to try to abridge this work; the result is less length, not better quality.

T41. —. "The New Cabinet and What It Will Do For Us," *Saint Paul's*, 3 (February, 1869), 538-551.

Identifying himself as a Liberal, Trollope rejoices at the recent election results, and defends the idea of fierce battle between the parties. He discusses the suggestions for plans for disestablishing the Irish Church, a move mandated in the elections. Tax relief and budget cuts are other pressing issues, he says, which must be carefully throught out before any action is taken. He notes also that there are serious administrative problems in the military which need attention. He comments on a number of members of the new cabinet formed by Gladtone.

T42. —. "President Johnson's Last Message," *Saint Paul's*, 3 (March, 1869), 663-675.

Trollope gives an account of U.S. President Johnson's political life, from his term as senator in Tennessee to his succession as President upon Lincoln's assassination. He describes Johnson's unpopularity with Congress, and summarizes the content of his recent final message to Congress. He remarks on the antagonistic tone and the futility of the "lame-duck" suggestions. Trollope asserts that Johnson might have done much good, and had a truly successful career had he not become President; as it is, he has "brought nothing but injury on his country, and nothing but obloquy on himself."

T43. —. "Mr. Disraeli and the Mint," *Saint Paul's*, 4 (May, 1869), 192-197.

Trollope objects strongly to the outgoing P.M. Disraeli's patronage placement of a secretary of his as Master of the Mint; this person was given the post over a man who by experience and good reputation had a much more legitimate claim to it. Not only is this action unfair to the man passed over, Trollope observes, but it is bad for the civil service system, and for the morale of the employees. Trollope finds that Gladstone's refusal to call back the appointment, once he became Prime Minister, is very regrettable.

T44. —. "Mr. Anthony Trollope and Baron Tauchnitz," *Pall Mall Gazette,* 9 (May 21, 1869), 1743.

In this letter to the editor, Trollope asserts that, despite a wide-spread rumor to the effect that he was engaged in a lawsuit against Baron Tauchnitz, the Leipsig publisher, he has never been, and is not now so engaged, nor is he contemplating such a suit.

T45. —. "Critical Notices," *Fortnightly Review,* 9 (June, 1869), 748-750.

Review of *Flood, Field, and Forest,* by Mr. Rooper. Trollope praises this as a book on field sports which is both interesting and well written. Unlike many previous works on these topics, this book has no "slang and frolic," but a great deal of helpful information.

T46. —. "The Irish Church Bill in the Lords," *Saint Paul's,* 4 (August, 1869), 540-555.

This article opens with a defense of the members of the House of Lords against the general charge that they are inefficient and undedicated, and thus very slow to act. Trollope discusses the issue of the Irish Church Bill recently debated and passed in the House of Lords, and remarks on the various arguments presented, the various difficulties and compromises required in framing the bill. He describes the bill which finally passed as better for all the debate and thought expended on it than it would have been had the first version passed quickly and quietly.

T47. —. "Formosa," *Saint Paul's*, 5 (October, 1869), 75-80.

Trollope summarizes and comments on the current public debate about a very popular play by Don Boucicault currently on the stage in London. The title character, a prostitute, is presented as both sympathetic and successful, and leading a happy life. Public demands for the play's closing because of its indecent subject matter have clashed with defenses based chiefly on the play's tremendous popularity with audiences. Trollope presents a reasoned defense for the depiction of criminals in literature and on the stage, with the proviso that their lives not be presented as happy and successful; such a presentation would be untrue as well as a bad example. On these grounds, Trollope condemns the presentation of Formosa in this play. He condemns authors, producers, and theatre-owners who allow fame and avarice to rule their artistic and moral decisions. Public demand or popular success is simply not a relevant consideration here, he asserts.

T48. —. Untitled editorial note, *Saint Paul's*, 5 (November, 1869), 214.

This is a brief critique of the preceding unsigned article proposing a wide-scale baby-care program, entitled "Babyland." Trollope thinks the cost estimates are far too low, and the level of care described would not in fact be practically possible.

T49. —. "What Does Ireland Want?" *Saint Paul's*, 5 (December, 1869), 286-301.

Trollope here argues that the Fenians, who want total separation of Ireland from England do not, in fact, represent all of Ireland, or even a majority. The Irish representatives in Parliament, he notes, have never suggested such a separation. There is widespread Irish support currently for the release of Fenian prisoners in English jails, and also a strong movement in Ireland for increased rights for tenants in regard to the land they farm. Trollope opposes both proposed changes, as not in the best interests of the parties concerned.

T50. —. "An Essay at Carlylism; containing the very melancholy story of a shoddy maker and his mutinous maid-servant," *Saint Paul's,* 5 (December, 1869), 292-305.

After praising Carlyle as a man, Trollope criticizes those of his self-styled followers whose doctrine is "simply, that we are all goint to the — Mischief!" This is a rather extended refutation on the notion that all people today are sloppier and less honest than was the case in former times. As the total population increases, the numbers of both good and evil people will increase. In answer to the implied criticism of fiction-reading as symptomatic of lowered standards, Trollope asserts that fiction is, when good, absolutely true, and not conducive to lowered standards of behavior. Good literature illustrates the truth that, in any age, to live a moral personal life is one's duty, and is in fact all that any one person has the power to do.

T51. —. "Mr. Freeman on the Morality of Hunting," *Fortnightly Review,* 6 n.s (1 December, 1869), 616-625.

Trollope answers an article by Edward Freeman which appeared in the October 1 issue of the *Fortnightly* criticizing fox-hunting as a cruel and inhumane recreation. Trollope notes that Mr. Freeman did not argue that hunters with guns or fishermen are cruel, though they also kill "innocent" animals.

He denies that hunters go out seeking personal pleasure through watching foxes suffer, and expresses resentment at Mr. Freeman's comparison of hunting with bear-baiting or bull-fighting. Trollope further argues that "cruelty" is never defined by Mr. Freeman, and might be charged against those who kill wasps, or creatures whose fur or shells they consider aesthetically pleasing. He insists that Freeman has exaggerated the pain of the fox, and underestimated the value of recreation. He concludes tht mawkish sentimentality is at least as serious as the "cruelty" practiced by fox-hunters.

T52. —. "Ancient Classics for English Readers," *Saint Paul's*, 5 (March, 1870), 664-668.

Review of Lucas Collins' English version of Homer's *Iliad* and *Odyssey*. Trollope points out that it is a good thing to know the plots of the classics, though not so good as to read them in the original. Versions such as these, true to the spirit of the originals, will be of use to the wide range of people who cannot read Greek and will not spend the time reading a literal translation. He admires the way that Collins has recast the story, described the monsters, and given a sense of the time of the original epics.

T53. —. "Mr. Gladstone's Irish Land Bill," *Saint Pauls*, 5 (March, 1870), 620-630.

Trollope notes with obvious relief that Gladstone's proposal for land reform in Ireland does not include fixity of tenure for tenants, which he [Trollope] has argued against in the past. He discusses Gladstone's abilities as an orator in convincing people of the merits of the new proposal. Trollope notes his points of disagreement with the proposed bill, and his hopes that it will be "locked into shape in Committee."

T54. —. "Charles Dickens," *Saint Paul's* 6 (July, 1870), 370-375.

Here Trollope opens with some personal reminiscences of his friend. He does not speak at length about Dickens' fiction; he notes that Dickens did break some of the literary rules, though he does not specify them. He observes that Dickens contributed a great deal to society; his writing changed people's lives, and his language added colorful idioms to the language.

T55. —. "Mr. Disraeli and the Dukes," *Saint Paul's*, 6 (August, 1870), 447-451.

Review of *Lothair*, by Benjamin Disraeli. It is clear in this review that Trollope has no respect for Disraeli either as a person or as a novelist: "We can only account for 'Lothair' by supposing that Mr. Disraeli has determined to satirize the aristocracy which has submitted itself to him, and the country, which for some months he certainly ruled, by palming off upon it as a work of genius a book purposely filled with every fault but one [indecency] of which a novel can be guilty." He continues, "Mr. Disraeli must have said to himself in his cynic solitude, – 'I will give them a story that shall be vulgar, ill-written, passing all previous measures in the absurdity of its adulation of rank, false as it can be made in its description of life, stuffed with folly; and even that they shall accept, – because it comes from me!'"

T56. —. "The English Aspect of the War," *Saint Paul's*, 6 (September, 1870), 562-571.

Here Trollope argues that, despite England's unwillingness to join in the Franco-Prussian War, the British should stand by the pledge made to protect Belgium. As things are going now, Trollope insists, England will not have to fight in this war; but it would be dishonorable to go back on the promise to Belgium, and such an act would devalue England's good name in the view of all the world.

T57. —. "Cicero as a Politician," *Fortnightly Review,* 21, n.s. (April, 1877), 495-515.

Of Cicero, one of his favorite historical figures, Trollope says, "his patriotism was so pure, so life-long, and so energetic, he was so specially clean-handed in an age specially defiled by corruption, and the records of his life have been left to us in language so charming, that I trust I may be borne with if I myself deal with the subject somewhat enthusiastically." He recounts the story of Cicero's career, focussing on the Roman's courage, honesty, and patriotism, and his "almost Christian" beliefs.

T58. —. "Whist at our Club," *Blackwood's Edinburgh Magazine,* 121 (May, 1877), 597-604.

This is a light-hearted account of how Trollope and his friends, all "well-stricken in years," gather each afternoon at about 3 p.m. to play whist for an hour or two. He notes that card playing is a great pastime for the old, as so many of the things they formerly enjoyed are beyond their strength, or are forbidden by doctors or family. At his club, he notes, his group is quite lively, and frequently startles the people in adjoining rooms by the loudness of their arguing and laughing. He relates several incidents to illustrate this, and concludes that the game would be boring to all members if they played quietly.

T59. —. "Cicero as a Man of Letters," *Fortnightly Review,* 22, n.s. (September, 1877), 401-422.

Trollope here writes for those unfamiliar with Cicero's works. He praises Cicero as speaker and writer, describing the power of the orations as clear and intense, both in content and to the ear. He urges his audience to read Cicero, and cites a number of the Roman's works which he especially recommends, detailing the subject matter and virtues of each.

T60. —. "Iceland," *Fortnightly Review*, 24, n.s. (August, 1878), 175-190.

Trollope recounts the story of a week-long trip to Iceland he made with a friend aboard the latter's ship, *Mastiff*. Trollope sketches a brief description of Iceland, including its history, climate, and the like. He relates his surprise at the high level of civilization he found there, considering its isolation. He had expected to find a much more barbarous people and much more public drunkenness. He notes that the little country does have hard times when ships carrying supplies are prevented by ice from delivering them, but this no longer happens very often. He describes some of the people he met and enjoyed, and an excursion he took to see "the Geysers," which were most impressive.

T61. —. "A Walk in a Wood," *Good Words*, 20 (1879), 595-600.

In this essay, Trollope begins by discussing his methods of constructing plots for his fiction. He recounts that he plans them mentally a section at a time, usually while on outdoor walks. He proceeds to describe the kinds of settings most conducive to thought. Many English woods are too domestic, he has found; the best places in the world are in Australia, California, and New Zealand. For the benefit of English readers, though, he notes several thought-inducing walking areas closer to home: parts of the Black Forest, and certain districts of the Duchy of Baden are particularly fine.

T62. —. "George Henry Lewes," *Fortnightly Review*, 25, n.s. (January, 1879), 15-24.

This is an obituary notice and appreciation of Lewes, who was the first editor of the *Fortnightly*. Trollope gives a brief biography, noting Lewes' careful research methods and the high quality of his writing and editing.

T63. —. "Novel-reading: The Works of Charles Dickens; the Works of W. Makepeace Thackeray," *Nineteenth Century,* 5 (January, 1879), 24-43.

Trollope discusses the nature and influence of novels, and sets some standards for both authors and critics. Novels are enormously popular, he notes, especially among the young; they are effectively replacing sermons as guides for behavior, both personal and social. Because of this great influence, novels should be written (or at least selected for reading) with great care. Virtue should appear to be a good, and vice to be base. Most of Defoe's works are bad because they do not do this. When a satirist of vice "lingers lovingly over the vice he castigates," it may be questioned how much good he does. The 'gothic' novels only make the imagination morbid; they do not teach anything worthwhile, he asserts. Trllope feels that Sir Walter Scott "towers among us" as a good example of novel-writing, being both realistic and moral. Dickens, he notes, while not always realistic, is always thoroughly moral. Thackeray has more life-like characters than Dickens, and teaches the same lessons as does the latter, Trollope observes. He feels strongly that any distinction between sensational and realistic novels is false; if a novel is good, it is both sensational and realistic — and if a novel is true, it cannot be "too" sensational. It is worth noting that this article was written after the *Autobiography,* which is often cited as the ultimate repository of Trollope's literary theory. This article comes down very stongly on the side of realism as the ultimate value in the event of a conflict between it and other values.

T64. —. "A Famous Novelist's Modes of Work," *London Society: An Illustrated Magazine of Amusing Literature for the Hours of Relaxation,* 44 (1883), 347-353.

This article consists of a brief introduction followed by a reprint of Trollope's essay, "A Walk in a Wood," as it appeared in *Good Words* in 1879. (cf. 761).

Bibliography

Booth, Wayne C. *The Rhetoric of Fiction.* Chicago: University of Chicago Press, 1961.

Haight, G. S., ed. *The George Eliot Letters.* New Haven: Yale University Press, 1955.

Hall, N. John. *Trollope and His Illustrators.* New York: St. Martin's, 1980.

Helling, Rafael. *A Century of Trollope Criticism.* Port Washington, New York: Kennikat, 1967.

Holcomb, Philip. "A Study of the Critical Responses to Anthony Trollope's Novels with an Annotated Bibliography of Criticism, 1920-1968." Ph.D. dissertation, University of Colorado, 1971.

Houghton, Walter E. "British Periodicals of the Victorian Age: Bibliographies and Indexes," *Library Trends,* 7 (April, 1959), 554-565.

—. *The Victorian Frame of Mind.* New Haven: Yale University Press, 1957.

—, ed. *The Wellesley Index to Victorian Periodicals, 1824-1900.* Toronto: University of Toronto Press, 1966+.

Irwin, Mary L. *Anthony Trollope: A Bibliography.* New York: H. W. Wilson Company, 1926.

Jones, Iva G. "A Study of the Literary Reputation of Anthony Trollope, 1847-1953." Ph.D. dissertation, Ohio State University, 1953.

Kincaid, James R. *The Novels of Anthony Trollope.* Oxford: Oxford University Press, 1977.

Marcus, Steven. *The Other Victorians.* New York: Basic Books, 1964.

Olmstead, John, and Jeffrey Welch. *The Reputation of Trollope: An Annotated Bibliography, 1925-1975.* New York: Garland, 1978.

Polhemus, Robert M. *The Changing World of Anthony Trollope.* Berkeley and Los Angeles: University of California Press, 1968.

Sadleir, Michael. *Trollope: A Bibliography.* London: Constable, 1928; Reprinted, London: Dawson's, 1965.

—. *Trollope: A Commentary.* New York: Farrar, Straus, & Company, 1947.

Skilton, David. *Anthony Trollope and His Contemporaries.* London: Longmans, 1972.

Smalley, Donald, ed. *Trollope: The Critical Heritage.* London: Routledge and Kegan Paul; New York: Barnes and Noble, 1969.

Snow, C. P. *Trollope: His Life and Art.* New York: Charles Scribner's Sons, 1975.

Super, R. H. *Trollope in the Post Office.* Ann Arbor: University of Michigan, 1981.

Trollope, Anthony. *An Autobiography.* Berkeley and Los Angeles: University of California Press, 1947.

Young, G. M. *Victorian England: Portrait of an Age.* London and New York: Oxford University Press, 1936. Reprinted, 1969.

Appendix A

Periodicals Surveyed for this Bibliography

Ainsworth's Magazine
Appleton's Journal
The Athenaeum
The Atlantis
Bentley's Quarterly Review
Blackwood's Edinburgh Magazine
The Bookman
The British and Foreign Review
Century
The Contemporary Review
The Cornhill Magazine
The Dublin Review
The Dublin University Magazine
The Edinburgh Review
Every Saturday
The Foreign Quarterly Review
Forum
Fraser's Magazine
The Galaxy
Good Words
Harper's New Monthly Magazine
The Home and Foreign Review
Knowledge: An Illustrated Magazine of Science
Literary World
Living Age
London Society
The London Times
Macmillan's Magazine
Manhattan
The Modern Review
Month
The Monthly Chronicle
The Nation
The National Review
The New Monthly Magazine
The New Quarterly Magazine
The New Review
The North American Review
The North British Review
The Nineteenth Century
Once A Week
The Oxford and Cambridge Magazine
The Pall Mall Gazette
The Prospective Review
The Rambler
Saint Paul's

The Saturday Review
The Scottish Review
Temple Bar
The Theological Review

Time: A Monthly Miscellany of Interesting & Amusing Literature
The Westminster Review

Appendix B

Entries Cited by Works Discussed

The MacDermotts of Ballycloran, (1847), 1, 118
The Kellys and the O'Kellys (1848) 2, 3, 4, 118
The Warden (1854) 5, 14, 18, 83, 118, 165, 188
Barchester Towers, 6, 7, 8, 9, 14, 18, 52, 83, 118, 165, 173, 188, 284
The Three Clerks (1858), 10, 11, 14, 18, 83, 165
Dr. Thorne (1858), 12, 13, 14, 18, 83, 116, 188, 266, 268
The Bertrams (1859), 15, 16, 17, 18, 19
The West Indies and the Spanish Main (1859), 20, 21, 22, 23, 24
Castle Richmond (1860), 25, 26, 27, 118
Framley Parsonage (1861), 29, 88, 118, 119, 120, 175, 186, 243
Tales of All Countries (1861), 31, 46
The Struggles of Brown, Jones, and Robinson (1862), 107
Orley Farm (1862), 28, 29, 30, 40, 41, 42, 43, 44, 45, 47, 61, 165, 175
North America (1862), 33, 34, 35 36, 37, 38, 39Rachel Ray (186

Rachel Ray (1862), 48, 49, 50, 51, 279
The Small House at Allington (1864), 52, 54, 55, 118, 119, 188, 243, 255
Can You Forgive Her? (1864), 59, 62, 64, 78, 118, 188
Miss Mackenzie (1865), 56, 57, 58, 59, 63, 151
Hunting Sketches (1865), 61
The Belton Estate (1866), 65, 67, 68, 71
The Clergymen of the Church of England (1866), 69, 70
Nina Balatka (1867), 73, 82, 235
The Claverings (1867), 74, 75, 76, 80, 119
The Last Chronicle of Barset (1867) 77, 84, 152, 175, 232, 243, 261
Lotta Schmidt and Other Storeis (1867), 81, 82
Linda Tressel (1868), 82, 235
Phineas Finn (1869), 89
He Knew He Was Right (1869), 85, 86, 87, 88, 102
British Sports and Pastimes (1869) 90
The Vicar of Bulhampton (1870), 92, 94, 96

The Commentaries of Caesar (1870), 97, 98, 100
An Editor's Tales (1870), 99, 102, 105, 163
Sir Harry Hotspur of Humblethwaite (1871), 103, 104, 106
Ralph the Heir (1871), 108, 109, 110, 111, 115
The Golden Lion of Granpere (1872) 112, 114, 117
The Eustace Diamonds (1873), 120, 121, 122, 188
Australia and New Zealand (1873), 123, 124, 131
Phineas Redux (1874), 127, 128 129, 188
Lady Anna (1874), 130
Harry Heathcote of Gangoil (1874), 132, 133, 134
The Way We Live Now (1875), 135, 136, 137, 138, 139, 140 143, 151, 152
The Prime Minister (1876), 141, 142, 143, 144, 145, 188
The American Senator (1877), 147, 148, 149, 150, 152, 153
South Africa (1878), 154, 155, 156, 161
Is He a Popenjoy? (1878), 157, 158, 159, 162. 164, 175
An Eye For An Eye (1879), 166, 168, 170
English Men of Letters — Thackeray (1879), 172, 174, 176, 180, 186, 259
John Caldigate (1879), 173, 175, 177, 178, 189
Cousin Henry (1879), 179, 181, 182, 183
The Duke's Children (1880), 185, 186, 187, 188, 189, 190, 191, 192

Life of Cicero (1880), 194, 196, 197, 198, 199, 206
Dr. Wortle's School (1881), 193, 195, 200, 204, 207
Ayala's Angel (1881), 201, 202, 203, 205, 207, 208
Why Frau Frohmann Raised Her Prices and Other Stories (1882), 209, 210, 215
Lord Palmerston (1882), 220, 221, 222, 223
Marion Fay (1882), 215, 216, 217, 219
Kept in the Dark (1882), 227, 237, 245, 246, 257
Mr. Scarborough's Family (1883), 258, 260, 262
The Land Leaguers (1883), 274, 284, 285
An Autobiography (1883), 264, 266, 267, 268, 269, 271, 272, 273, 275, 277, 279, 281, 282, 283, 300
An Old Man's Love (1884), 285, 286, 287, 288, 290

Appendix C

Entries Cited by Selected Topics

Americans, 33, 34, 35, 36, 37, 38, 147, 148, 149, 150, 152, 186
Austen, Jane, 2, 55, 235, 238, 247, 299
Balzac, Honore, 75, 204
Braddon, Miss, 113, 128, 246
Bronte, Charlotte, 242
Browning, Elizabeth Barrett, 293, 294
Bulwer Litton, Edward, 93, 95, 298
Black people, 20, 21, 22, 23, 154, 155, 156, 161
Black, William, 246
Carlyle, Thomas, 293
Clergymen, 5, 6, 7, 8, 9, 30, 47, 49, 53, 57, 67, 70, 84, 89, 90, 95, 113, 118, 219
Collins, Wilkie, 47, 101, 118, 121, 157
Dialect, 26
Dickens, Charles, 18, 56, 93, 95, 108, 118, 128, 167, 190, 210, 236, 240, 243, 248, 266, 281, 289, 297
Eliot, George, 19, 50, 101, 118, 128, 130, 145, 190, 242, 243, 244, 248, 295, 300
Female Characters, 34, 41, 45, 49, 50, 54, 55, 62, 64, 78, 80, 92, 97, 103, 104, 112, 122, 133, 144, 148, 164, 170, 202, 237, 256

Ferrier, Miss, 235
Fielding, Henry, 290
Gaskell, Mrs., 298
Haste of composition, 10, 11, 13, 19, 35, 124, 154, 164, 207, 217, 222, 259, 261, 300
Humour, 1, 2, 3, 23, 64, 86, 94, 110, 147, 178, 185, 193, 207, 211, 213, 215, 227, 272, 273, 280, 287
Irish People, 1, 2, 3, 26, 89, 165, 274, 284
Kingsley, Charles, 95, 133, 134
Law and Lawyers, 5, 11, 13, 19, 41, 43, 53, 56, 58, 175
Length of works, 12, 15, 34, 36, 121, 123, 124, 139
Male Characters, 61, 62, 65, 69, 70, 78, 93, 97, 122, 127, 144, 151, 159, 215, 285
Melville, Herman, 118, 247
Mudie's Library, 18
Morality of works, 5, 11, 42, 44, 47, 48, 49, 50, 52, 54, 59, 92, 94, 122, 130, 136, 137, 159, 162, 164, 166, 167, 169, 170, 178, 185, 252, 271, 282
Narrative method, 18, 20, 27, 54, 63, 257, 261, 289
Newspapers, 8
The Orient, 15, 23

Ouida, 246
Payn, James, 246
Periodicals, 31
Plot, 5, 6, 9, 10, 13, 16, 27, 29, 30, 61, 62, 65, 68, 86, 117, 149, 164, 174, 181, 202, 204, 262
Railways, 17
Reade, Charles, 71, 93, 115, 289
Richardson, Samuel, 279
Sand, George, 269
Scott, Walter, 125, 190, 281
Sequels, 6, 29, 30, 77, 144, 185
Thackeray, William Makepease, 10, 11, 19, 29, 49, 50, 55, 60, 93, 95, 108, 118, 122, 125, 128, 140, 157, 167, 172, 176, 180, 190, 203, 235, 241, 242, 246, 281, 290, 302
Theology, 16, 26, 66, 118
Trevelyan, 268
Trollope, Frances, 1, 33, 93, 113, 283, 296
Turgenieff, Ivan, 265
Setting, 15, 17, 26, 41, 114, 117, 118, 133, 211, 214
Woods, Mrs., 47, 113, 246
Yonge, Miss, 49
Zola, Emile, 190, 302

Appendix D

Entries Cited by Authors

Alford, H., 69
Austin, A., 280
Bristead, C. A., 108
Broome, F. N., 88
Bryce, J., 247
Capes, J. M., 14
Chorley, H. F., 1, 2, 6, 72
Collyer, 109, 135, 143, 147, 154, 158, 166, 172
Cook, 185
Cunningham, H. S., 44
Dallas, E. S., 8, 18, 23, 24, 50
Dicey, A. V., 128
Dixon, W. H., 40
Donnelly, T., 32
Edwards, A. B., 254
Escott, T. H. S., 165
Freeman, E. A., 244, 248
Gwynn, S., 301
Hamley, E. A., 39
Harrison, F., 300
Hawthorne, J., 275
Hoey, J. C., & F. C., 89, 118
James, H., 60, 64, 65, 261
Jeaffreson, J. C., 48, 52
Jewsbury, G., 5, 11, 12, 15, 25, 76, 79
Johnson, E., 283
Kinnear, A. S., 53
Knight, J., 75
Lewes, G. H., 42
Macleod, D., 279
Maine, H., 10, 13
Meetkerke, C., 252, 280
Meredith, G., 9
Morley, H., 153
Morley, J., 271
Oliphant, M., 80, 92, 242, 253
Payn, J., 289
Peck, H. T., 302
Percy, G., 83
Pollack, W. H., 259
Reade, C., 115
Roscoe, W. C., 19
Sedgwick, A. G., 290
Sergeant, 173
Shand, A., 151, 281
Stack, J. H., 84
Stewart, C., 61
St. John, H., 6
Tanzer, A., 273
Taylor, H., 91
Towle, G. M., 93
Ward, M., 271
Washburn, W. T., 55
Wedgewood, J., 290
Whitehurst, E. C., 282
Wilberforce, 68
Wise, J. R., 73, 77, 86, 97, 102, 107, 198

Appendix E

Entries Cited by Publication

Appleton's, 87, 93, 138, 146, 150
Athenaeum, 1, 2, 5, 6, 11, 12, 15, 25, 28, 33, 40, 48, 52, 68, 72, 76, 79, 109, 112, 132, 135, 141, 143, 147, 154, 158, 166 172, 173, 179, 185, 193, 201, 206, 209, 211, 217, 222, 227, 236, 258, 267, 274, 286
Blackwoods, 39, 80, 92, 116, 161, 169, 196, 252, 272, T58
Bookman, 302
Century, 261
Contemporary Review, 69, 71, 290
Cornhill, 42, 289, T1, T2
Dublin Review, 32, 89, 118, 256
Dublin University Magazine, 37, 47, 58
Edinburgh Review, 151, 281
Every Saturday, 95, 126
Fortnightly Review, 61, 75, 84, 91, T5, T6, T7, T8, T9, T10, T11, T11, T12, T20, T21, T25, T27, T28, T29, T30, T31, T45, T51 T57, T59, T60, T2
Forum, 300
Fraser's, 36
Good Words, 242, 279, T61
Harper's, 259
Knowledge, 239, 241
Literary World, 101, 106, 117, 121, 129, 131, 139, 142, 152, 160, 162, 163, 167, 168, 171, 175, 176, 183, 184, 187, 188, 199, 207, 215,140, 250, 251, 254, 257, 265, 277, 283, 288, 291, 294
Living Age, 248, 249, 253, 276
London Society, T64
Macmillan's, 244, 271, 301
Manhattan, 246, 275
Month, 243
Nation, 60, 64, 65, 128, 190, 247, 273
National Review, 19, 44, 83
Nineteenth Century, 153, 189, T63
New Monthly Magazine, 4, 17, 38
North American Review, 55, 108
North British Review, 45, 53
Once A Week, 113
Pall Mall Gazette, 57, 70, 78, 82, 98. 115, 157, 180, 191, 194, 202, 212, 216, 221, 224, 225, 226, 228, 229, 230, 231, 233, 234, 237, 238, 255, 263, 269, 278, 293, 295, 296, 297, 298, 299, T3, T4, T13, T14, T15, T16, T17, T18, T19, T22, T23, T24, T26, T44
Rambler, 14
Saint Paul's, T32, T33, T34, T35, T36, T37, T38, T39. T40, T41, T42, T43, T46, T47, T48, T49, T50, T52, T53, T54, T55, T56
Saturday Review, 7, 10, 13, 16, 20, 26, 29, 31, 34, 41, 46, 49, 54, 56, 62, 66, 67, 74, 81, 85, 90, 94, 99, 104, 111, 114, 122, 124, 125, 127, 130, 133, 136, 145, 148, 155,

159, 170, 178, 181, 186, 195,
197, 203, 210, 213, 219, 220,
235, 260, 270, 284, 285
Temple Bar, 380
Time: A Monthly Miscellany, 165
The London *Times,* 3, 8, 18, 23, 24,
35, 43, 50, 63, 88, 96, 100, 103,
110, 120. 123, 137, 144, 149, 156,
164, 177. 182, 200, 205, 214,
232, 264, 266, 268, 287
Westminster Review, 9, 22, 27, 30, 51,
59, 73, 77, 86, 97, 102, 105, 107,
119, 134, 140, 174, 192, 198, 204,
208, 218, 223, 245, 262, 282, 292